strategies in
humanistic education

volume 1

tim timmermann

&

jim ballard

$5.95

a mandala book

table of contents

mandala is an educational and organizational consulting group. we offer pre- and in-service training courses and workshops in the area of humanistic education, for teachers, nurses, recreational directors, etc. where people are working with people, we have an interest. our communication and problem-solving labs and workshops have been attended by people from across the nation. we are especially interested in informing you about these activities. you may receive a current calendar of events by writing to mandala.

preface

the intent of this volume (and the ones like it that follow in the series) is to spark your interest to create humanistic-education activities for the students in your classroom.

we have selected a series of words that are important to the process of living and growing. using these words as stimuli to our thinking, we've generated activities and ideas for use in the classroom.

we are eager for you to try these ideas and to write to us about your outcomes. we would like to be informed of ways you've found to upgrade or successfully adapt the strategies for special needs, levels or settings. also, we welcome suggestions for new activities that might be included in future volumes of this series (we promise to credit you by name). our future plans include the publication of at least four additional volumes, along with an annual yearbook on humanistic education.

for more information, write us at mandala. we hope to hear from you.

tim and jim

introduction

books for educators tend to fall into two categories: the theoretical and the practical. the first group is needed in order that educational systems and processes be constantly scrutinized, that new and innovative models be explored—that our sights be raised beyond what-is to what-could-be.

the second group tends to be of more immediate help to teachers, because books of this type offer concrete suggestions for implementing immediate changes in learning environments. this book is of the second type. we think of it as a sort of cookbook in humanistic education, in that it offers a variety of approaches that fulfill the following conditions:

- they deal primarily with the affective realm of living and developing—the realm of feelings, thoughts, values, wishes, and attitudes, as well as with behaviors and skills.
- they are structured, and derive from specific objectives.
- they can all be done in the classroom.
- they allow for flexibility as to time you can afford.

format

the book is designed with the busy person in mind, and thus the format is extremely simple, that of a reference book. basically, there are two parts to the book, the *how-to section* and the *activity section.*

the how-to section

here are presented specific skill clusters which the teacher will use over and over again in conducting the activities presented in the activity section. the *activity section* is keyed to the *how-to section* so that you can constantly refer to the latter section in planning certain activities, the way you would use the reference section of a cookbook that presents information on the various cuts of beef, as you are preparing to follow a recipe in the book for "boeuf au jus."

2

the activity section

this is the "recipe section" of this book. here is the variety of classroom activities through which your students can experience the humanistic learnings you value.

in the activity section you will find a group of twelve words that represent concepts or constructs. these serve as thematic headings under which are grouped a variety of classroom activities.

bias

the matter of sexism in language needs treatment here. when writing about "people-in-general", it is difficult to prevent the appearance of sexual bias in mere wording. the authors have chosen to (a) try to avoid phrasing that feeds into perpetuation of sexist stereotype, (b) include as many 'he/she' choices as possible, when referring to the individual person, and for the rest, (c) where it is natural and appropriate, alternate the traditional "he" or "his" which has come to connote "human" in standard writing with "she" or "her". we ask our readers to understand that we are sensitive to this issue.

philosophy

there is a strong philosophical system underlying our *strategies* series, and it is presented here in outline form. basically, the ideas in this book rest on the following broad assumptions:

- people are okay; that is, humans are vitally important, worthy of caring, respect and trust.

- people are their own greatest resource; the seeds of growth and solutions lie inside the grower/problem-solver.

- awareness of self is essential to choosing responsibly.

- each of us can be nicer to himself/herself than he/she tends to be.

- each of us is responsible, and we are always choosing, in any situation, who to be.

- fear is our major limiter.

- behavior arises out of needs.

- alternatives for meeting needs can always be found or generated, then chosen.

the how-to section

here is a list of skills and strategies that are included in this section:

- the s-i-s-f model

- brainstorming

- circletime

- discussion methods

- journals

- 6-point continuum

- role-play

- small-group methods

- fantasy

- processing

- w.u.b. worksheet

refer to this section whenever you need to, to conduct the activities in the *activity section,* many of which are keyed back to the items in this section. vary the methods according to group needs, time limits, and your own intuition.

5

the s-i-s-f lesson plan model

here is a model or format for any learning experience, which we feel strongly is most facilitative of achieving learning objectives. the plan is our substitute for the kinds of motivations that have traditionally led to stultified school experiences: authority, punishment, reward, or conformity. we call it the *s-i-s-f* model because it involves four steps: structure, involvement, success, and feedback. this is a plan that can be instituted in carrying out *any* classroom activity you choose; and we have tried to include strategies in this book that follow this model. whether your lesson plans call for lecture, dynamic small-group work, creative activity, rap, seatwork, drill or whatever, if any one of the steps in the s-i-s-f lesson plan model is omitted, there is less likelihood for real learning to proceed. here is what we mean by the four steps:

structure—the planning, setting-up and adhering to specific guidelines, usually by you, the teacher. teachers tend to be comfortable with providing structure. the issue as far as learning is concerned is: structure for what? structure can take the form of directions, rules, seating arrangement or a worksheet outline—anything from "i want you to take out your ecology texts and turn to page 19", or "number off 1-2-3, please", to "spend some time getting yourselves together in groups of five and arranging your chairs in circles" or "please get comfortable and close your eyes to get ready for a quick guided fantasy-trip." structure provides the framework for the activity, sets limits, provides expectations, etc. most important is that it is somehow a structure that *leads to* . . .

6

involvement—the participation by choice of students, their own voluntary including of themselves, *in terms of their own personal concerns.* involvement means doing, acting, initiating, responding, participating as an important entity, a person with an indispensable role, in the process of learning. it is the very opposite of having something *done to,* or *for,* the learner. if the initial structure has been right (i.e. has been such as to funnel the learner into the involvement stage), this portion is usually characterized by bodies that move, faces that are alert, a sense that there is not very much difference between the task-doer and the task itself. involvement that has been carefully structured-for and that, by its very nature, takes up or carries along the learner, will be involvement that in one way or another will *lead naturally to . . .*

success—a sense of satisfaction, of accomplishment, of "i-*did*-it!" (or "we-did-it!"). this may or may not include the experience of "winning", in the self-enhancing, non-competitive sense—as when the outcome is a product of which the maker is proud. for sometimes what we call success is simply the *very being involved* in that special way that a child is involved when he or she is truly learning something that *makes a difference* for him or her. thus, an "i-found-out" fits our definition of success just as much as an "i-did-it." of great importance to us in helping teachers design success experiences for youngsters is that the success be evaluated as such primarily *by the doer,* rather than by some external evaluative source. the part you, the teacher, play in this kind of experience emerges more in the final stage, for you have somehow been able to arrange this experience so that the learner feels that his success is earned. it is genuine it is not a phony giveaway. it had sufficient challenge, and the challenge was *felt* at the involvement state. also, the experience is such that you the teacher, or someone else that is there, can *easily provide . . .*

7

feedback—some means for the child of gathering information from what he did; *that* he did it and *how* he did it. we are talking at this stage about something of a factual or descriptive nature that enables *him* to focus on his learning behavior, evaluate it as worthwhile. this, then is the difference between a teacher's saying "nice job, marie!" (making the outside agent the evaluator, and setting up a one-up and one-down, judge-and-judged, dependency-promoting relationship) . . . and the teacher's saying "i see that you mixed blues and greens in this part of your painting" or "looking at those colors gives me a cool feeling about your painting" (providing information in such a way that the recipient feels noticed and/or appreciated, and can better see what and how he did). there are always two viable alternatives to evaluative feedback, both of which are more effective and enhancing of growth: one is *descriptive* ("i saw you . . .", "you have done . . .", "i notice your . . .") and the other is *appreciative* ("i like . . .", "when you ———— i feel . . .", "i'm uncomfortable with your . . ."). also, feedback should be varied; it may be spoken, written, mirrored in expression, solicited from peers. the teacher is not the only feedback-giver for the success or involvement.

if you buy into the s-i-s-f model, try writing those four letters in each block of your lesson-plan book for a week, and see if you can arrange for all four steps to take place for your students in whatever you have planned for the period or day. people who have learned to use the format skillfully have found that it nearly always has these outcomes:

8

1. it puts the emphasis on learning, rather than on teaching.

2. thus, it puts the emphasis on learners, as the "stars"—and on teachers as facilitators of learning.

3. it seems to provide for more surprise, spontaneity and discovery, to everyone's enjoyment.

4. because of the order of events (i.e. structure that is there *in order to lead to involvement* and success), it channels a teacher's energies more effectively and satisfyingly than if the order were random or non-involving for kids (i.e. structure that is imposed merely to enforce authority or keep the lid on).

5. it reduces win-lose competition between teacher and student, and student and student.

brainstorming

the rules of any brainstorm are simple. it is useful to post them and review them before beginning a brainstorm:

do's

• make as long a list as you can

• record everything

• go far-out—nothing is too wild

• "piggyback" (borrow on ideas)

don'ts

• no rights, no wrongs, no evaluations

• no discussing, questioning or defending any item

before presenting any of the activities under any one topic heading, first spend one or two days' sessions brainstorming the topic head as described below; then move into the activities under the heading and stay on that topic for awhile, as in the unit approach.

brainstorm a definition   write the topic word or phrase on the board, with the word "is" after it (as in "anger is . . ."). then ask the class to give *other names* for anger. show that you want, not examples but definitions. become the "scribe" for the class, and encourage them, through you as a writer, to fill up the board with other words for the topic. these need not be single words. in fact, once you have made the task clear, be entirely uncritical of what comes, and write it all down. if someone is off task, let the group police them back. write everything given, but if other things than definitions, are given (i.e., examples), write these off to one side. at the end, have the group tell why you wrote them separately.

brainstorming examples   again, write the topic word and "is" on the board. this time, you want the class to call out, as allegorical definitions, examples from their experience. give a few examples to get them started, and remember that items tied to the world of the senses tend to be more powerful and meaningful.

you might say:
    "close your eyes and listen as i say some words
    that some people used when they thought about
    what anger is . . .

    anger is the feeling in my head and shoulders when someone
    breaks something of mine

    anger is my arm coming up in the air, to hit

    anger is falling down

    anger is when i'm blamed for something i
    didn't do

    anger is the red inside the black inside of my eyes . . ."

at first, be content with responses such as "anger is what i feel when . . ."; as groups learn to do this push for more direct, metaphorical statements. make or have made a copy of the brainstorm responses before you erase the list, since many uses can be made of them (some are suggested in the activities).

other brainstorms   beyond these kick-off approaches, a brainstorm is an enjoyable, productive activity almost anytime. some other brainstorms are suggested in the activity section, but you can create your own—often out of the real-life problems that arise in the classroom. thus, there can be brainstorms of class rules, solutions to conflicts, guidelines

11

for sharing discipline, approaches to educational problems, debriefing, evaluating, winding-up or processing any activity, etc. it is important, if productive storming by your students is to go on unhampered, that you follow these guidelines as leader:

- ask for single-word or single-phrase items this encourages everyone to participate, and makes your writing task easier.

- model the desired skill of *acceptance of ideas without evaluation,* inasmuch as possible. if something is bothering you, say so; otherwise, no editing.

- be a gatekeeper only on the processes of the brainstorm—not the content. make sure you *write it down in the kids' own words.* more than any other behavior of yours, this tells children their contributions are worthy and accepted as given.

- where necessary (group or individuals are off-task, someone is showing off through his contributions, or material is otherwise irrelevant), group off-the-track items as you write them, keeping that list separate from the one you want.

- do not be hesitant, every so often, in contributing items of your own. (this can sometimes work as a "steering strategy" for guiding the group into desired areas of thought).

example of brainstorm results

two of us brainstormed this list as ways to get people involved in the process of learning. you will come up with many more ways.

circletime
debate
movie

news article
canvassing
science fiction

interview
skit
monologue
tv
dialogue
diary
job chart
collage
experience chart
retreat
street interview
guided fantasy
unguided fantasy
brainstorm
role play
skill practice
reaction sheet
soap opera
show and tell
bring and brag
small task groups
inner/outer circle sharing
simulations
trust games
group games

6 point continuum
dyads
support groups
fish bowl
panel
news cast
puppet shows
shadow shows
non-verbal practice
board games
vtr
audio tape
t-group
design games
process models
assigned readings
observation
here/now wheel
research projects
seed sentences
cassettes
ingredients packet
at-home activity
programmed texts
rap sessions

writing ideas

poem
song
script
essay
journal
diary
from-standpoint-of
titles

book
editorial
bumper stickers
letter
billboard
value card
telegram
fill-in-blanks on cartoon

headlines
news article
greeting cards
notes
extemp paragraphs

comic strip
record jacket
container copy
commercial jingles
limericks

circletime*

a *circletime* is an activity which can be carried on with a group of children numbering from 5 to an entire class. it is designed primarily as a small-group experience; ideal-sized groups go from 5 (at levels pre-school through second grade) up to 12, (sixth grade and beyond). usually seated in a circle, the teacher and children spend from ten to twenty minutes a session, communicating around a topic. readily distinguishable from a discussion or rap session, circletime focuses each session on a new segment of common human experience. the major goals of a circletime are (a) to foster self-awareness in children, and (b) to build skills of effectively sharing and listening to feelings.

the rules of the circletime, repeated each session at the beginning, are:

- everyone gets a turn who wants one

- everyone who takes a turn gets listened-to

these rules focus on the communications processes through which the activity builds skills of sharing and listening. the second rule, by example of the teacher and gradual in-volvement of the kids as the routine way of responding, becomes defined in practice as "everyone who shares gets *feedback,* on a here's-what-i-heard-you-say basis".

following the review of the rules, the teacher gives the task for the day, and the interaction begins. here is an example of a partial circletime "script":

teacher: today we're going to think about *"a time i was lost."* think of a time you were lost. were you lost from somebody? was somebody lost from you? were you alone?

*this activity is much more fully described as an entire year's curriculum of affective growth for each grade level, in our publication entitled **circlebook.**

15

	how did it happen? and, (very important) how did it *feel* to you?"
karen:	well, i got lost last summer, at the beach. a man had to bring me back to my mother. i was scared.
teacher:	thank you, karen. can anyone tell karen what she has shared with us?
alice:	last summer you were on the beach and got separated from your mother. you were scared. a man brought you back to your family.
karen:	right.
teacher:	alice, you listened to what karen said and what she felt. is there anyone else who wants a turn?
todd:	my dog had to find me once . . .

interaction countinues as long as people want turns, including
the teacher. the above script is given here so that
you can note the kind of response the teacher is making.
when todd is through talking, the teacher or another student
will tell him back what he said—in her own words and *in a way
that tells todd his feelings were heard.* there is no questioning
("was that at night or during the day?"), no commenting ("i
know what you mean because i had an operation once . . ."),
no directive response at all. the reason (beyond mere time
restriction) that responding modes are thus limited becomes
clear when the *primary goal* of circletime—*building self-
awareness*—is considered. in this model—a kind of 'listening
laboratory' for the world of feelings—it is the *speaker's* needs
to be listened to that take priority. therefore, responses are
generally limited to *mirroring.*

mirroring is in some ways easy to do, and in some ways hard. it is easy in that it takes pressure off the listener to try to think of what to say next, after the speaker is through talking— which is what we are usually doing. it is hard in that it puts pressure on the listener to stay entirely focused on the person of the speaker, to give place, to let the other carry the ball. there is difficulty sometimes in feeding back the right feeling-message. sometimes the listener "misses"—but no one gets hurt. the speaker knows you are trying to listen. he or she will feel grateful for your attention and quite willing to correct if your listening is 'off'. use words like the following to give mirroring responses:

in other words . . .

you felt . . .

sounds like . . .

seems like you're saying . . .

i hear that you . . .

you didn't like it when . . .

it's important to you that . . .

in circletime, everybody practices communicating feelings by saying "i" (when it is my turn) and responding with "you" (when it's yours.)

each new heading in the activities section includes a variety of circletime topics related to the theme. feel free to vary these, and add more of your own. (some 300 such tasks appear in the *circlebook*.)

17

discussion methods

a discussion can be an effective learning experience—or it can be a turnoff for kids. many teachers teach largely by discussion, whereas others rarely use this tool in the classroom. analysis of classroom interactions where much discussion takes place (i.e., where the teacher is comfortable with discussion as a teaching style) reveals that often the teacher is talking much more than the students—and does not know it.

as with any learning activity, the key question seems to be: how much are kids *involved* in terms of their own concerns? the reason that many classroom discussions prove deadly for learners is that the model we call a 'discussion' is little more than an invitation for the talkers to talk and the listeners to listen.

how can discussion be made more engaging, effective and facilitative of learning for all kids? here are some suggestions:

1. if possible, *start with a "discrepant event"*, such as a catchy sentence, a roleplay presentation a group has previously prepared, a picture, a behavior—something that calls attention in a slightly jarring way, something that 'makes heads turn' a little. focus attention. letting something dynamic initiate a discussion builds far more motivation than "now let's talk about . . .".

2. *structure for quick, easy responses by everyone.* this can be done by placing an issue statement ("reading is a better use of time than watching tv") on the board and asking for one-sentence responses; or by using a sentence stem ("if i had a million dollars . . .") and having each student write out a response before sharing—or doing a 'whip' by going around the class in order, having each child complete the sentence

aloud or say "pass". dynamic elements may be introduced by forced-choice statements ("would you rather be a famous surgeon or a famous athlete, if you had to be one?"), and even asking kids to divide by standing at one side of the room or the other before making motivational statements.

3. *don't be afraid of silences,* be aware of who talks more— you or the kids. practice economy of words yourself. try to make your comments only the needed ones—be open-ended and facilitative. model listening rather than talking. give time to ponder and wonder.

4. *no easy answer,* or *no one right answer.* you will involve more of the group if it is evident from the outset that all contributions will be encouraged and protected from judgement. where there *is* only one right answer, use another technique for learning than discussion. a discussion should never be a public exercise for dividing winners from losers.

5. when the material under discussion lends itself to a *dip into a more personal dimension,* use such questions as:

when did *you* feel the way betsy in our story did?
what would *you* have done?
has anything like this every happened to *you*?
want to tell about a time *you* had somebody do that to *you*?

some teachers do not value asking questions like these, for their concern is that the "material won't get learned" if kids take time to relate to it by sharing this way. but it is precisely *when* children enter this dimension, make this connection between 'outside-me' and 'inside-me', that we can say they are *learning.* there is a certain leap of recognition when this happens. you can help it happen by being alert as a discussion leader to help kids make the direct personal confrontations that bring growth and self-understanding.

6. *maintain a facilitator or moderator role.* demonstrate your neutrality. encourage contributions by reflecting what kids say ("in other words, lucy, you're saying that there doesn't seem to be an easy way to keep younger brothers or sisters from tagging along with you and your friends?"). responses by you that clarify what contributors say are valued by all; they show respect and interest on your part. sum up the ideas the group generates, using the chalkboard or a flipchart to record. gain consensus, when you can, on issues that affect the entire group. above all, *listen!* your demonstration of listening skills will do far more to encourage growth, learning and risk-taking than will your own inputs—even if you know the answer or know how to "say it better."

7. *allow for non-closure.* just because kids don't have "the answer", don't think learning and involvement aren't happening. stop discussion when the group's *energy* peaks, *not* when the answer is reached. if a child or a group of children "earns" their answer, they'll be more responsible with it. value the struggle, value open-endedness for its own sake. support the search, the rummaging, of learners. delight in their discovery.

8. *process* the discussion. deal with here-and-now thoughts, feelings and behaviors by occasionally stopping to ask things like:

> what does it feel like to do this?
> how do you feel now, that's different from when we started?
> what kinds of things do you find yourself thinking about here?
> are we on or off the subject? how can we get back?
> what do we want to do with this, as a group?

after the discussion is completed, process it by asking:

> what were we just doing?

20

what did you have to know or do to be in on that discussion?
are you satisfied with where we came out?
what did we want from that discussion? did we get it?

also, use the techniques of debriefing and evaluating described in the "processing" section, just ahead.

journals

journals are usually ongoing classroom diaries of personal experience that may or may not be shared with the teacher and/or others. you can have children make and decorate their own, use ditto'd handouts that become pages in the journal, use notebook forms—whatever suits you. periodically, allow 10 to 20 minutes for students to write in their journals. (journal entry topics in this book may be drawn from the *circletime* topics given. also found near the beginning of each unit heading in the activity section are specific sentence beginnings or "stems" for the children to complete.) you can use a variety of approaches to journals—for instance, having some entries drawn instead of written. there should be common understanding from the first about *what is* shared from journals and *how it* is shared. because of the personal nature of this activity (sometimes children who rarely talk at all will write a great deal of revealing things in journals), you should respect and enforce what is decided regarding who reads journals.

if, as is common, the teacher periodically collects the journals for reading, be sure to write comments in all books—if not all entries—to show that you have read them. this can become an exhausting task, so limit it from the beginning, or be ready at any time to announce: "i need help! i can't respond to all the things you're writing." on the other hand, if children are sharing little of themselves, trust needs to be built; perhaps the sharing guidelines need revision. basically, journals are for kids, not teachers. it is the self-awareness that comes through responding on paper to an affectively-oriented task that is the objective here.

6-point continuum

this is an engrossing activity that can involve kids at 5th grade level and beyond. it is usually done in small workgroups of 5 to 8. each group's task is to create a model of a continuum with six points designated as position-points on some issue. for instance, say that our group has chosen "attitude toward the environment". the product of 20-40 minutes of group work might look like this:

(attitude toward the environment)

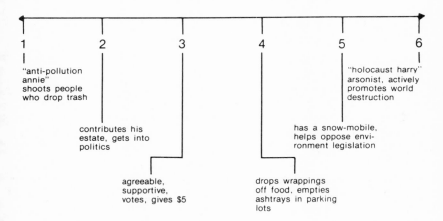

this is an activity that requires considerable skill in working with ideas. suggest, before or as groups work, these guidelines:

—develop opposite endpoints first. label them as ridiculous extremes.

—as your group works to fill in the other 4 positions, be thinking about where *you* stand on this continuum. then, help develop a position statement out of that place.

23

—keep noting the space left to work as you progress; and make sure each point differs from the rest.

some ways to use the products of a continuum session:

—post around the room and share

—make individual scorecards, with numbers that correspond to the continuums posted. kids walk around and give numbers for where each stands. cards may be shared, or not.

—reproduce the continuum on a ditto, have students fill in where they stand. enter in journals.

whether it is called for or not in a given thematic area in this book, you can have your class or a small group make up a 6-point continuum from any of the themes presented. for instance, in a case such as "patriotism", think both positive and negative (patriotism / unpatriotism, or love of country / hatred of country, etc.) in order to create the endpoints. be sure to *make these endpoints difficult to identify with,* by making them ridiculous extremes. this forces each person to make a decision to take a place somewhere on the continuum that is not just an easy either-or choice. depending on your group's maturity level, you might create one or two continuums yourself and use them with the class before asking them to create their own.

remember that the real experience of awareness expansion comes with the individual's responding and committing to something. thus, the continuums you or the class make will exist as means toward self-knowledge. always push for the kids to take a stand publicly, to place themselves on the continuum, to show where their values are. and, be sure to do the same yourself.

use continiums in your classroom for 5-minute sharings, writing the endpoints and entering initials of volunteers who will tell where they fell on the spectrum. example:

how do you keep your room?

←◄ 1   2   3   4   5   6 ►→

"messy moe"
junk all over;
garbage rotting;
can't find his
bed . . . governor
is about to de-
clare moe's room
a disaster area.

"spick-n-span
sonja"
catches dust
as it falls;
folds dirty sox
before putting
in hamper;
you could "eat
off the floor."

role-play

children are natural role-players, and we can learn from them
how it's done most effectively. in the most effective and
productive of roleplays (those that create most self-awareness
in the role-player and learning for process observers) there
seems to be a combination of

—playing the role of the person or type assigned
—at the same time, being one's own feelings

if you can encourage children in roleplay to *play someone else*
but simultaneously *be themselves,* you will facilitate more
learning in the activity. this means, then, that a person
playing a role of someone of a very different age or
background or type would assume that role, and then go
ahead in creating the interaction without always stopping to
think: what would so-and-so do or say? instead, encourage
role-players to enter into the *feelings* of the role.

no great acting ability is called for in roleplay. there is no
script; this is spontaneous interaction. there is no ex-
pected outcome either, no game-plan the players have to
follow. they are simply playing at being someone else in
another situation. who they are, what they bring to the roleplay in the raw material of feelings, thoughts and personal
values, is the stuff of the roleplay.

it may be hard to get this point across to students who wish to
evaluate their own or others' performance levels. work at it;
use roleplay often, and they will become more comfortable
with "playing someone else, and being yourself".

some additional guidelines for roleplays:

1. be specific about who's-who in the roleplay, but give little more in the way of background than role, age, name and sex of the person being portrayed.

2. keep roleplays short (1 to 3 minutes).

3. assign observers to watch for specific elements (evidences of emotion, tone, pace, body language, etc.), and not simply be entertained.

4. vary format between practiced, performance-type roleplays, and unrehearsed roleplays (usually more effective in terms of spontaneous, here-and-now learning).

5. after stopping the roleplay, allow the players to share their feelings first, then observers to tell what they saw or heard.

6. process the roleplay both on a "what" and a "so-what" level. that is, deal both with what-we-saw-happening-here and how-this-is-like-us-in-real-life-situations. (see the section on processing skills for additional ways to deal with the roleplay after it is over.)

7. always focus attention more on the *behaviors and feelings* generated during the roleplay, than on acting ability or specific outcomes.

small-group methods

small groups have some of the greatest educational payoff of any kind of interaction there is, and yet teachers traditionally make little or no use of them beyond "reading groups" at lower elementary level. the dynamics involved in any small group are so numerous and operate so quickly that there is usually enormous energy on tap. the problem for leadership is to turn the energy to best advantage for learning. hence, small groups for the classroom should be mostly *task*-groups. the directions for organizing the groups, the task and the time limits must be made clear at the outset.

the dyad

a dyad, or partnership of two, is often the best way to process an activity, discuss a topic, or practice an interaction skill. as soon as you create partnerships, you have automatically created a structure for the greatest amount of simultaneous interaction your class can conduct. there can be no takeover of talkers, or withdrawal of listeners. simultaneously, fully half the people in the room can talk at once, quietly, and be attended to very well.

dyadic tasks should be short, and should allow time for processing. thus, you could conduct a listening-skills laboratory for 15 minutes this way:

"group b (half the class) choose partners this time. you have 1 minute. try to pick someone you haven't had a partnership with before this. "a" will be first to talk to "b"; "a" is talker, "b" is listener, then we'll switch. "b", your task is to be able to tell "a" his or her feelings back, after "a" is done. "a", your task, beginning when i say "go" and for 1 minute, is to tell "b" about your favorite season of the year—why you like it, how it feels to you. any questions? go . . . stop! now, "b" tell "a"

28

what you heard—especially include "a's" feelings. go . . .
stop. now switch, and "b" tell "a", for a minute, about *your*
favorite season; get into your feelings about it. go . . . stop.
"a" feed back "b's" feelings. go . . . stop. now, talk for a
minute together with your partner about what it was like to be a
speaker in this practice, and what it was like to be the listener."
(afterwards:)" now, what partnerships would like to share with
the group some single words or short phrases that describe for
you what it was like to be the speaker? the listener? thank
you."

beyond skills practice, the dyad is a good way to process
something: "give yourself a number between one and ten
that tells how you feel about that last activity; zero is awful,
10 is fantastic . . . now, tell someone next to you your
number." "partner for the day" or "partner for the week" is a
good way for each kid to feel connected to someone, and
you can give frequent opportunities for partners to discuss
things and do the process tasks you want if dyads work well
with your class. you can use them as 3-minute "changes of
pace," utilizing the *circletime* topics or journal entries from the
activity section as sharing tasks.

larger groups

group size is an important factor to an activity. little kids
operate well in groups of 4 to 8, if the task is to be largely
verbal (as in circletime), while older groups can get along
well with from 8 to 15. remember this simple rule-of-thumb,
though, when thinking about the interaction you want: *as
the number of participants in a group goes up, the opportunities for each to participate go down,* and children
begin to use power roles to get the attention they want and
need ("power roles" of course include not only the
dominator but the dominatee).

seat groups in circles whenever possible, to maximize interaction and observation. other guidelines to utilize, depending on your objectives for the group:

—appoint leaders. these can simply be "pickers", who call on whoever in the group is raising a hand to talk next; or they can be facilitators, to keep the group on task; or they can be reporters, to report in the large group about the outcomes of their group's work—or all of the above.

—in leaderless groups, make sure everyone gets a turn by

- assigning "pass-around" tasks (example: everyone tells in turn "something i like to do").

- asking groups to stop and consider who has not talked and give them a chance

- the introduction of a talk-ticket (holder of this object is the only one who can talk) or a timer or stopwatch to limit interactions

—always respect the feelings of those who don't wish to talk by introducing the pass-option. children will not be put on the spot if they know they can simply say "pass" and the spotlight will move away.

—create some choices for the group to make so that they "own" the task more. place several discussion topics, continuum topics, circletime topics or debate topics on the board and say to the groups "spend the first two minutes deciding as a group which topic to use for the next half-hour".

—reduce resistance to quitting when you call "time" by giving a 3- or 1-minute warning signal.

—have the groups *process* themselves. this is very important—perhaps more important than the accomplishment of the task itself. give some time at the end of each group to discuss questions like the following (if you don't want them to discuss, or haven't time, simply say the questions and ask them to 'think' the answers):

how do you feel about being in this group today?

how do you feel about your group's accomplishment of the task?

how did you feel toward me as the task-giver and time-keeper?

which did you do most in the group—talk or listen?

who talked the most? who listened? how did people show they understood?

what role or roles did you play today? leader? follower? humorist? peace-maker? withdraw-er? other?

would you like to do this again? different task? different people?

what would you do differently with this group today if you had the task to do over again?

what was your "high" and what was your "low"?

fantasy

structured opportunities for fantasy, both guided and unguided, are excellent means for providing enrichment in the classroom, changing the pace of the day, training imagination, and facilitating the building of self-awareness in your students. everyone fantasizes, daily. structured fantasy experiences legitimize dreaming or day-dreaming, and teach that imagination is a priceless resource in creating unique solutions to problems and generating novel and aesthetic products.

the fantasies, like all other activities presented in this book, are not to be thought of as "therapy" but as means of developing awareness and building skills essential to education of self. the teacher's role in the structured fantasy experience is that of setting the guidelines for the fantasy. specific guidelines, as directions to the class, can include:

- closing eyes and / or putting heads down on desks; being quiet

- focusing attention outward—to noises in the room, temperature of the air, sensation of the texture of desk or chair or floor, etc.

- focusing attention inward—to breathing, to relaxation of muscle groups, to "the movie screen on the backs of the eyelids"

- guiding the fantasy with specific directions ("let yourself see a sun-drenched meadow . . . go and be in it . . . feel the warm breeze on your cheek, smell the fragrances of many blossoms . . . now hold out your hand, and find in it an object that reminds you of a favorite time in your life . . . now open your eyes gently, and turn to a partner and share whatever you would like to share out of this experience")

- helping children to share or process the fantasy

guided fantasy—like the example above—is perhaps most helpful when it includes opportunities (as this one did) for students to *create* things in their imagination. an effective tool for guided fantasy is the method called "take yourself away and bring yourself back". group children in threes, have them close their eyes and "take yourself away to a favorite place of yours . . . be there for awhile, just enjoying that favorite place . . . see things in color . . . smell smells . . . hear the sounds of your place . . . now, bring yourself back, and open your eyes. share with your partners where you went." you can have students "take themselves away" several times in a row between sharings, each time introducing some change, such as weather, temperature or atmosphere of their place, a person or object to find there and bring back, etc.

another easy guided-fantasy format is the one suggested in richard demille's book entitled *put your mother on the ceiling.*

quiet recorded background music is an excellent means of helping create a relaxing atmosphere for a fantasy.

unguided fantasy is an opportunity for the child to make more of his own inputs, umhampered by your directions. what is important here is to help set the stage. you might, for instance, open by having students see themselves on a mountain, by the ocean or in a meadow. after quietly and gently guiding them part way, say "now, feel free to wander, to go where you want, and to do what you want, for the next few minutes . . ." after 3-5 minutes have elapsed, gently say, "figure out how to get yourself back into this room in the next minute or so."

always end a fantasy experience by inviting students to share whatever they wish to share, either with a partner, a small group, or the class. many of the suggestions in the next section on processing skills are appropriate here.

processing

in one sense, we have been discussing processing all along. the list on page 31 is an example of processing an activity. in fact, what we are calling affective education or humanistic education could also rightly be called "process education", for it involves a continual looking at the "how" of human behavior. in school, there tends to be great emphasis on the "what", the stuff of learning. *how* something is learned may be (probably is) more important than the something it-self. for instance, as a teacher i can teach a child both to *do* math and to *hate* math, at the same time; his attitude toward math will be just as telling as (may even determine!) his use of math in the future. thus, education to feelings, attitudes and values is an essential part of the learning process. the processing techniques presented here attempt to make this awareness happen in the midst of, or immediately after, an experience.

this list of process questions, like the foregoing one in the small-group section, will give you an idea of what interventions you can make in simple ways to raise children's consciousness of themselves and of others:

during the exercise:

- *what is going on* right now?

- how do you *feel* about what is happening?

- *if you* (the class, the group, someone else) *were* a (color, kind of weather, animal, tv character or show, other object), what would you be? why?

- what was the last *thought* you just thought?

- become aware of how your *body* feels right now.

35

- where are we in terms of the *task?*

- what do you *want?* (a very confrontive, but non-blaming, process question—often useful, during a discipline problem to cause a student to give an account—not of his/her *behavior*—but of her/his *motivation* or *objective* in causing a disturbance).

- how can we get where we want to *go?*

- what does the group *need* right now?

- *if i said* ———, how would you feel? (time for a break, stop, let's work 30 minutes more on this, you don't have to finish, etc.)

- if you were to *give a title* to what's happening, what would it be?

- what would it *take* to . . .

- how would you *respond* if i . . .

- what *role* do you see yourself playing right now? (refer to a list of roles group has identified on a chart)

- *write down a word* that tells what you are feeling (collect, have shared, or   ?)

- draw a *here-and-now wheel* like this one. in each space, write the name of a feeling you can find inside you right here, now. star one of the feelings, and write a statement about it at the bottom. example:

* i'm anxious because i don't think our group will finish in time.

- decide where you are on this *continuum* (place on board a continuum with points that speak to some process).

- *discuss with a partner* for three minutes your feelings about the activity, and be ready to share in the large group.

(obviously, many of the above may be used as a followup debriefing or critique of the activity)

after the exercise

- respond on paper to any of these *sentence-stems* on the board that are appropriate to you:

i learned ———— (to, that, that i, that others . . .)

i was most comfortable about ————

i was most uncomfortable about ————

i wish ————

i wonder ————

i wanted more (less) ————

- *collect "highs" and "lows"* from the activity

- *thumbs up* (if children like the activity they hold thumbs up; if not, thumbs down. if neutral, make a fist. i feel strongly, circulate thumbs in air. all do this at once, and look around for instant "fix" on group reaction)

- *journal entries* (journals make excellent ongoing process records; have students write entires, using one or another of the methods here, after an activity from this book, or after a test or lesson from the content curriculum)

- *yay-book* (teacher names various aspects, or steps in the sequence of the activity, and students all whisper loudly either "yay" or "boo" according to how they feel about it.)

worksheet in upgrading behavior ["wub"]

this strategy is attributable to gerry weinstein of the university of mass.; it has been adapted from his "trumpet" model.

the purpose of the activity is to identify a *behavior pattern* that the behaver wants to change or upgrade. it is best used after a dynamic, involving activity that represents a "confrontation experience"—one in which a person behaves by *reacting* or *responding* to a situation in a fairly (for him/her) predictable way.

(an example—which might be used in class to teach the "wub" model—is announcing to the class, as if by a sudden decision, "i need eight volunteers for something". do not tell the class what you need volunteers for, even if asked, and simply wait until you have them. then, stop, thank whatever volunteers responded, and begin to process the behaviors by asking kids to tell—or, better, write down—exactly what they thought, felt and did in the "volunteering" situation.)

pass out copies of the "wub" worksheet to the class and "walk them through" the process, explaining each step, answering questions, and allowing time to fill in the blanks. the more public this process is, and the more examples shared at each step, the more understanding will result of how to use the "wub". below is the model for the worksheet, and following it are things you might say in explaining each step.
(examples from the volunteering situation are given here for *your* understanding, but would not appear in the blanks on the worksheet).

directions (spoken or written, to accompany the first walk-through of the "wub"):

1. write down exactly what you could see yourself doing.

2. fill in "is" or "isn't" depending on whether what you just did is what you *usually* do; complete step 2.

3. step 3 has several blanks to fill in; all of them are about "payoff"; the things you get by behaving the way you do.

4. step 4 is looking at *what you want that you can't* get because of your pattern.

5. now it's time to *weigh the good against the bad* in your pattern. imagine that the things your pattern *gets for you* are on one side of a balance scales, and the things your pattern *costs you* are on the other. see if you can decide "which weighs more".

6. if you checked the first blank in step 5, do not go on. if you checked the second, then step 6 is a chance to *name a new and different behavior* that would get you more and cost you less. try to imagine something *small* in the way of a change—small enough to insure success, and encourage you to develop a new pattern with greater payoff, out of it.

the "wub" worksheet has countless uses. hand out copies after a particularly high-involvement activity, after a test—or after a fight breaks out. keep a stack of copies on hand "for all occasions." the worksheet, given to a single child in a counseling setting, can show caring and produce insights. create your own uses.

worksheet in upgrading behavior

1. i just _did not volunteer_
   (*what i did*)

2. when in this kind of situation, this
   (___✓___ is _____ isn't) what i usually do. my
   pattern is to _not volunteer, look away._
   (*what i usually do*)
   when _someone asks for volunteers_
   (*situation*)

3. my pattern gets me _off the hook_
   (*payoff—what your pattern gets for you*)
   because of my pattern, i can _hide_
   and i don't have to _be in the spotlight_
   my pattern helps me _stay safe_

4. however, because of my pattern, i don't get
   to _learn from risking, help the group_
   (*cost—what your pattern keeps you from getting*)
   my pattern costs me _understanding of self_
   i have to give up _knowing what it's like_

5. it feels to me as if my pattern:
   _____ gets me more that it costs me.
   ___✓___ costs me more than it gets me.
   therefore, i (___✓___ do; _____ don't) want to change
   my pattern in some way, so as to get more
   and give up less.

6. instead of _hanging back_ , as i've been
   (*pattern*)
   doing, i think that _occasionally volunteering_
   (*new behavior*)
   would be more satisfying to me. something i
   could try next time _someone calls for a volunteer_
   (*situation repeated*)
   would be _to raise my hand if I'm_
   (*name different behavior here*)

sure I'm not going to be made a fool of.

41

the activity section

this is the "recipe section" of this book. the twelve headings group the activities into themes or units. you are the best judge as to what pace or sequence to follow here, and as to how to fit the various recipes to your setting, needs and style.

we have not attempted to gradate the activities at all, in terms of age or grade level of students. instead, we present these activities as ideas which you can tailor to your students' needs. the way they are introduced will depend upon your own methods of effectively adapting each recipe.

the *sequence* of activities is also entirely up to you. (as you examine the list of themes below, decide which appears to be a likely starting-point for your group.) we present each topic in a uniform format that *suggests* a sequence. for instance, each topic begins with a list of purposes, and suggests a brainstorm session with the class to define the topic and give examples of it to afford identification with the theme. our recommendation is that you begin the treatment of each topic in this way.

next come the circletime tasks, journal entries and discussion starters. these are to be used at your discretion, interjected at regular but appropriate times—*not* all at once, as·it might seem is suggested. these items, together with the list of activities that follow them, are to be "mixed and matched" to your liking. it is at this point that each topic becomes a list of classroom activity recipes—and, as with cooking, there are endless combinations possible for any one classroom's "menu".

here is the list of 12 themes:

acceptance	joy
needs	courage
self-concept	intimacy
risk-taking	death
change	celebration
patriotism	anger

acceptance

purposes

- to promote understanding of the importance of acceptance as a common human need

- to facilitate awareness in a student concerning which of his and others' behaviors are acceptance-seeking behaviors

- to help students accept themselves more

- to widen the range of alternative behaviors for giving and gaining acceptance

acceptance

definition

brainstorm "acceptance is . . ." in small groups—for both definition and examples—and compile a master-list ditto handout as an insert for journals or a committee-made bulletin board on acceptance.

discussion starters

- what sorts of *behaviors* (what you can *see* a person doing) show acceptance and non-acceptance on the part of a person? group? from includer (-ee) and excluser (-ee)?

- what *words* show acceptance? non-acceptance?(give examples)

- what other parts of a spoken message *besides words* show these? (tone, loudness, pace, intensity, etc.)

- what kinds of things can we do to make another person feel accepted? not accepted?

- what things *about us right now* can we talk about that have to do with these themes? (i.e. language, dress and hair styles, physical distance from each other, who participates, etc.)

- are acceptance and love the same? how are they different? (acceptance and trust? acceptance and friendship?)

acceptance

circletime topics:

- something in someone else that i don't accept

- how i gain acceptance from people (peers, adults, etc.)

- i (someone) kept someone (me) out

- i (someone) included someone (me)

- a time i feel (felt) really accepted

- the difference between being acceptable and accepted

journal entries

- i gain acceptance by . . .

- i show acceptance by . . .

- the most accepting person i know

- what it takes for me to feel accepted by someone

- i feel most accepted when . . .

- i feel most unaccepted when . . ..

- my list of "unacceptables" (situations, behaviors, types of people, etc.)

47

activities

☆

skits: take volunteers from the class who will agree to act out a skit. have them choose a topic from the following list:

> being new
>
> i was chosen last
>
> breaking into a group
>
> someone kept me out
>
> someone showed me acceptance when i really needed it

have the group (4 to 5 students) spend a class period planning the skit, distributing parts and rehearsing. the next period, have them present the skit, having assigned the rest of the class to be "videotape cameras" to record and be able to "play back" behaviors of those in the skit. after the skit, discuss the behaviors and apparent feelings of each person, his or her role, motivations, etc. focus last on the person whose part represents the cue or story from the above list that the skit group chose, and have several class members volunteer to tell when *they* have felt like this character.

☆

blue eyes and brown eyes: watch "eye of the storm" replay on cbs "60 minutes", by yourself or with the class, as available (or send for film).
conduct a similar experiment with your entire class or a small group. that is, designate a trait (such as eye or hair color, height, etc.)—*or* make a name tag-like item to be worm—that separates class into two distinct groups. have one group be the "acceptable" group, the other the "unacceptable" group. switch roles at mid-day (or at next class period). process the feelings carefully afterwards.

acceptance

acceptance in song: this theme is a frequent one in pop
music. have a committee collect phrases or entire songs from
the current hits which illustrate people's need for acceptance.

have group break up into *task forces to* take the tune from
some popular song and write new words around the acceptance theme, then sing or present the song.

☆

"breaking in". one child volunteers to be on the outside of a
circle of about 12 kids, to try to break in. the rest lock arms and
stand in a tight circle, doing all they can to deny the 'outsider'
entrance. he or she attempts, by whatever means, to get inside
to the center of the circle. after a round or two of this, change it
so that there are two 'outsiders' to a round, who may collaborate.
afterwards, discuss feelings, both of those on the outside as well
as those in the ring.

☆

additional discussion topics: what are some ways we *gain* or
earn acceptance from others? what ways have worked for
you? not worked? when have you been on the inside, and
helped keep someone else out? differences between un-
conditional acceptance and "conditional" ("you're-okay-if")?

☆

how do *animals* show acceptance, non-acceptance? list
body and facial clues in communicating acceptance, non-
acceptance?

☆

make *individual lists* of "things i don't feel accepting of, in

49

acceptance

myself". then make lists of "things i don't feel accepting of, in others". ask students to compare lists, and to share any "i-learned-that-i" statements with a partner.

☆

pantomime: have small groups spend a period composing and practicing short non-verbal skits around the acceptance theme; another period presenting them. ask each group to plan how to moderate a class (audience) discussion following their presentation of the skit.

present these guidelines before the groups meet:

theme: acceptance

possible titles or subjects: i was accepted, i was unaccepted, i felt unacceptable because of my ————, i thought they wouldn't accept me, i wouldn't accept myself, i didn't accept someone, etc.

time: 3-5 minutes

discussion format: compose 3 questions pertinent to the skit, and use them to structure discussion. be sure to make one of the questions on the *personal* level (related to those in the audience directly). examples:

what things did marcia do to gain acceptance?

how could you tell through 'body language' that tom felt unaccepting?

when have *you* felt this way (done this)?

☆

acceptance collages: have 2s or 3s use pictures from re-cycled newspapers and magazines to create collages

around the theme. collages could assume special shapes
(example: cut large—24" x 36"—block letters out of
tagboard, and have each group create its collage on one
letter. then, mount the letters on a bulletin board.)

☆

contract: this activity involves 3 steps: (1) becoming aware of
one's style of gaining acceptance; (2) processing that style
to determine whether it needs upgrading (i.e., a change to a
different behavioral style to achieve more desirable results);
and (3) sharing the desired change with a partner and
contracting with that partner for the change. the activity
may perhaps best be spread over three different days or
periods.

step (1) may be achieved in a number of ways: roleplay entitled
"what i had to do to gain acceptance"; a game like "breaking in";
etc. here is one suggestion in addition:

allow several kids—or, if possible, the entire class—an opportunity to spend 15 minutes in another classroom, with a
group of significantly different age or grade level. this visit is to
be conducted not as a group, but individually, (set up this
visitation schedule with other teachers, in advance, and devise a
rotation schedule with passes, so as not to disturb other building
routines). immediately afterward, have each write a paragraph on
the experience, focusing on (a) writer's *feelings* in that strange
environment, and (b) writer's *behaviors* out of those feelings.
(these might also be done effectively in brainstorm-list form.)

experience, focusing on (a) writer's *feelings* in that strange
environment, and (b) writer's *behaviors* out of those
feelings. (these might also be done effectively in brainstorm-list form.)

acceptance

step (2): next, assign the "wub" worksheet, in order to help kids get in touch with their styles of gaining acceptance. have them enter the behaviors from (b) above in step 1 of the wub, and continue.

step (3): partners now meet to contract with each other on desired behavior changes. use this contract form:

I, ——————————, agree that next time i want to gain acceptance with another person or group, i will not

———————————————— as I've done in the past, but

instead i'll ——————————. if i do this as

agreed, i promise to reward myself by ————————

——————, and to report results to my partner ———

————————————

——————————————————————
signature

——————————————————————
"notary"

make sure each partner makes a contract, and that partners both "notarize" each other's forms and agree on a reporting means and deadline.

☆

brainstorm: conduct a total-class or small-groups brainstorm on "additional tasks around the acceptance theme that we'd enjoy." then, design and have fun with the new curriculum.

52

needs

purposes

- to enable students to identify needs as sources of behavior

- to have students appreciate the variety of needs different people have

- to have them understand that people behave out of unmet needs

- to make them aware of their own individual styles of expressing or fulfilling needs

needs

definition

brainstorm a definition of *needs*. then, brainstorm a list of *kinds* of needs; help keep this broad by introducing the brainstorm with "people have a need to (for) . . ."

discussion starters

• present the different need levels devised by maslow (see *toward a psychology of being*, maslow, a.)

• does need imply weakness? strength?

• the world's greatest need—what?

• all behavior comes from a need—agree?

• when there is a needs conflict at home our family usually ———

• if you were stranded on a desert island what three things would you want besides food and water? rank-order them in importance.

circletime topics

• how i get what i need

• a time i told someone i had a need

• what teachers need

• i know others need things when ————

• something someone does that i don't understand but that must arise out of a need

54

needs

- a need i could fulfill in another person

- something i think you need is — — — —

journal entries

- how i get what i need

- what boys need from girls

- what girls need from boys

- what children need from parents

- what parents need from children

- what teachers need from students

- what students need from teachers

- one thing which i really need that i don't get very often

- i *don't* need — — — —

needs

activities

☆

brainstorm the different ways peoples might resolve a need
conflict. (*examples:* teacher needs order on a rainy day, while
kids need to use pent-up-energy . . . two spouses need their
one car, each for an important event . . . two friends wish to
see different tv shows . . . etc.)

☆

watch a tv soap opera in class and list all the ways you see that
characters in the drama get their needs met. do *you* use any of
those ways? which ones? how can the same identical needs be
met in *other* ways?

☆

what needs are being met by:

watching a football game
playing football
sleeping late
skipping class
'putting down' someone
buying a new car

biting your finger nails
saving money
having kids
joining a club or organization
making a friend
others

☆

brainstorm the different ways people might resolve a *needs
conflict,* in such a way that *both* parties get what they need:
examples to kick off the storm might be:

you and a friend prefer to see a movie together, but differ
on which movie to see.

56

needs

you and a brother or sister both need to use a bike at the same time.

you are sharing a room with someone, one of you is very neat, the other sloppy.

you are riding in a car with someone who is smoking, and the smoke is bothering you.

☆

tape-record a party or dinner at home. *analyze* in terms of how people get what they need.

☆

all of us need:

attention
acceptance
approval
affection

brainstorm the possible ways to get these things.

☆

do a six-point continuum on the concept of *meeting needs:*

aggressive_____submissive

place yourself on the continuum.

have others in your small group tell you where *they* think you are on the continuum.

needs

☆

create a *need box* where students can anonomously make needs known to you. even though you won't know who has the need, you may be able to adjust the environment to fulfill the need. (alternative: the box is periodically opened and class brainstorms solutions to each expressed need.)

☆

note to teacher: where a conflict arises in your classroom, take time to *define the problem in terms of needs* of each party, rather than "who started it, "who's right or wrong, who's stronger or more manipulative, etc.

☆

have students *create a consulting service* among themselves. have each of them suggest what service they could individually or collectively provide, such as:

math computation
advice on something tutoring help with a hobby.
"listening"
what else?

provide time that they can consult with their counselor(s). create a system of payment in which all can participate such as:

free time
goodies
tokens for books etc.

needs

☆

have each student make a *needs collage.* (if you have not introduced class to maslow's hierarchy-of-needs model, do so at
this time; encourage students to include items from each of the
need levels in their collages.)

☆

have students help you move all the furniture and other things out
of your room so that nothing remains but blank walls and floor.
then, begin to move things back in that group feels are really
needed. (be ready for decisions to eliminate some items.) help
them to label the things according to maslow's hierarchy such as:

we need seats ———— *physical comfort*

art work ———— *beauty*

each other ———— *belonging*

☆

make a list of all the things you did today. tie each of them to
maslow's hierarchy.

example:

lunch ———— *physical*

p.e. ———— *physical*

discussion with a friend ———— *belong,* etc.

☆

have each student list "20 needs of mine". then guide them in coding each need according to the following need categories:

p ———— *physical*

s ———— *safety*

s ———— *security*

b ———— *belonging* [*social*]

e ———— *esteem*

u ———— *understanding*

b ———— *beauty*

have the class help you enlarge on the coding system by suggesting other needs not covered in this list (i.e. the need to create, to escape, to assert oneself, to fulfill one's destiny, to have integrity, etc.)

self-concept

purposes

- to help students realize that their perceptions of the world have much to do with the way they feel about themselves

- to promote more positive self-concepts in children

- to build awareness of the fact of others' self-concepts and of how these impinge upon interactions with the self

- to build skills of self-affirmation

self-concept

definition

tell the three-men-and-an-elephant story: three blind men
came upon an elephant. one began to feel the elephant's leg,
and soon announced: "an elephant is like a tree." the second
felt the elephant's stomach and said: "no, an elephant is like a
big boulder." "you are both wrong," declared the third, feeling
the elephant's trunk, "an elephant is like a snake!" which man
was right? were all right? wrong? how does focusing on only
one aspect of something keep us from seeing what its essence
is?

apply the same learning (about facts, or "percepts"—i.e.,
single perceptions—as against entire bodies of facts as
contained in notions, or "concepts") to the self. explain that it
does not make sense to define oneself as one's fingernail,
tongue or elbow—or, more abstractly—as one's creativeness
in music, one's friendliness, one's fear or one's anger.

begin to push to more inclusive definitions with a "self-
concept is. . ." exercise, by supplying one or two items
yourself (example: "self-concept is all that i believe about
myself").

next push for *examples* by using the sentence-stem "self-concept
is involved when . . ." (example: "self-concept is involved when i
blow it.")

self-concept

discussion starters

- what can you tell about a person's self-concept by the way he or she walks? talks? dresses? makes choices? etc. (stress the tenuousness of such perceptions, also)

- who made (makes) *your* self-concept? (this is usually a process of others first—in infancy—and the self later.)

- how does a person *change* the way he or she sees him (her) self? how have you?

circletime topics

- a time i feel most okay about myself

- a time i feel foolish

- something about myself i don't understand

- how i put myself down

- something i like about myself

- something i don't like about myself

- a wish i have to be different somehow

- a way i have of telling myself i'm okay

- what i'd be like to live with (have for a friend)

self-concept

journal entries

- when i like myself i usually . . .

- when i don't like myself i usually . . .

- things i like about myself (list at least 20)

- things i don't like about myself (list at least 10)

- something about myself i could be more accepting of

- i get my idea of who i am and what i'm like mostly from:

———— things i do   ———— who i look like

———— things i think   ———— my body

———— things i feel   ———— how others treat me

———— my values   ———— mistakes i make

———— what others say ———— things i do well

———— successes and ———— other (what?)
failures
———— what i look like

activities

☆

private-office inventory: have students rate themselves on the following items, using the following rating scale: 1—super-okay; 2—okay; 3—okay/not-okay, or not sure; 4—not-okay; 5—super-not-okay

—— age   —— dress

—— sex   —— habits

—— color of skin, eyes, hair   —— friendliness

—— height   —— neighborhood

—— weight   —— popularity

—— physical appearance   —— smartness

—— athletic ability   —— possessions

—— money   —— part of town, or town

—— religion   —— grades in school

—— ethnic background   —— artistic ability

show students how to average their numbers (there are 20 items in the list). without sharing their "average numbers", have them talk about how a self-concept is formed. ask: is the number you came out with as an average from this (partial) list of indicators accurate as far as how you feel generally about yourself? how can we change our self-concepts? (show that self-concepts are continually "under fire" from self-percepts; that we continually choose, act, and *assess the action*—and thus gain another perception of ourselves.)

self-concept

☆

have students choose partners they like, trust and feel
comfortable with. put the following list on the board (or on
handout sheets), and have each take time to complete two
lists—one for how he or she feels about him/herself, and the
other for how he or she feels the *partner* feels about
him/herself. then, have them read the lists to each other,
checking each item out together. (reinforce the pass option
for all or any of this.)

☆

self-concept inventory this may be done as a journal entry—or
as an anonymous handout/handin, the results tabulated and
shared as a "class self-concept."

place an x on the line where you see yourself in each case:

smart ————————————————	dumb
beautiful ————————————————	ugly
strong ————————————————	weak
likeable ————————————————	unlikeable
fast ————————————————	slow
leader ————————————————	follower
alone ————————————————	with others
okay ————————————————	not-okay
acceptable ————————————————	unacceptable

self-concept

☆

the 1-2-3-4 game: seat the kids in foursomes, with four slips of paper—marked 1, 2, 3 and 4 respectively—in each group. at your "go" signal, each group has one minute to negotiate for shares in an imaginary dollar. play at least four rounds of this, with each group keeping its own "score" (how much money each player accumulates); a new dollar is hypothesized for each round. the key notion to explain is that the numbers represent *shares of power* (i.e. 4 has four times the power of 1, etc.). make sure the groups understand these rules before starting:

1. numbers are to be reshuffled and picked "out of a hat", at random, each new round.

2. players must *collaborate* to get money, by *combining shares the total either six or seven.* (go through the possible combinations with the class: 4 can combine with 2, 4 with 3, 4 with 1 and 2, or 1, 2 and 3. the way the game is set up, someone is left out of the money each round.)

3. *who gets how much* must be decided inside of each 1-minute round, or else *no one gets anything.* players must "wheel and deal" within the minute, and those who decide to use their powers—either the shares of power on the paper they drew, or their own powers-of-persuasion—to combine for portions of the hypothetical dollar, must have combined their papers and held them up, before you yell "stop".

process. after the game, reconvene the entire group and talk about feelings and behaviors during the playing. have the class brainstorm the "feelings of a 1" by listing feelings, through you as writer, on the board that were connected with drawing the number 1 slip of paper. do the same for the three other numbers.

self-concept

finally, use the four brainstorm lists as resources for a discussion on "shares of power in the real world". ask: "what number list stands for the way you feel when . . . (you're new in town?"; . . . you win a prize, or a game or race?; . . . you bring home your report card?"; . . . you go to a dance?" . . . you get compared to a brother or sister?"; etc.)

an alternative is to have students share *in what situations* they tend to feel "like a 1" (powerless) or "like a 4" (powerful), etc. *major learning:* many times our feelings, good or bad, in a certain situation have to do with how much *power* we feel there—power to negotiate decision-making, to get our way, to share in rewards, etc.

another approach: ask: "what do people *do* when they feel like a 1? a 2? a 3? a 4? what do they say? how do their faces look? how do their bodies look? how do they walk?" follow up with partnership roleplays (example: "who would like to roleplay a 1 and a 3 both heading for the same parking space?")

☆

have everyone do the "private office inventory" described above. afterwards, have each average his scores, to come out with a *number that tells how i feel about myself.* give the following "questions to think the answers to": were you surprised at how your number came out? if you can recall having drawn that same number during the 1-2-3-4 game—and the feelings of having that number—what does this tell you about your own feelings of power to negotiate with others for what you want out of life?

☆

have each student make an anonymous list: "five things i don't like about myself;" and then: five things i like about myself;" and hand them in. questions following the listing: which list was easier to make? why do you think this is so? as you think

68

self-concept

of the items you listed, do you think anyone else in the group might have put down the same or a similar thing?

the next day, present on ditto copy to the entire class a compilation of the items. show how many people mentioned each thing (nose—5—too short, too long, too big, wrong shape, etc.).

questions following the compiled handout: do you find your items on the list? did your predictions about others come true? how does it feel to find out that others listed the same or similar things? to find out what others listed that you did not?

ditto the self-concept circletime topic list as a handout, but with long blanks after each item. give kids a period to write responses, explaining you want no names on them (tell them they may disguise their writing, print, etc.). after collecting them, have a committee create a bulletin board entitled "feelings about me" and post the papers or large printed excerpts from each, for all to read. (before they write, explain what you plan to do with the papers, and ask any who do not wish theirs to be used in the display to put "no post" at the top.)

creative writing titles: place on board, ask kids to choose one title and write a story, poem, song, tv script, diary entry. or other:

i thought i was the only weirdo

the only me i've got

feelin' okay

feelin' not-so-okay

if i were 3 people talking together

☆

good what? play the game "good what?" by having kids arrange themselves in circles of 3 to 5. say: "i am going to say some phrases, each beginning with the word *good.* you are to think about yourself—think whether or not you are what i say. for example, if i say 'good friend', you will think: 'am i a good friend, usually?' if you decide you are, you'll say *yes* when your turn to respond comes round. say *no* if you think you are *not* a good friend, or say *pass* if you're not sure, or if you don't wish to share. okay, here we go. *good friend.*"

allow time for each to have a turn to respond out loud to the others in her/his group. then repeat the following, pausing each time for the sharing. (an alternative to verbal sharing is to have each write *yes* or *no* responses privately.)

good student (pause)
good game-player
good son or daughter
good brother or sister
good organizer
good fighter
good peace-maker
good worker
good dreamer
good dresser

good writer
good talker
good leader
good listener
good teacher
good follower
good thinker
good looker
good dancer
good singer

start the game by directing it yourself, then ask each group to pick it up on their own and go at their own pace, making up their own phrases.

☆

in some way afterwards, *process* the feelings associated with
the game. relate outcomes to previous learnings about self-
concept.

variation: allow time, if necessary, for those who wish to tell
why they chose as they did (this is particularly a temptation
when one votes 'no', and can be enlightening for others in the
group). the choice to tell why is also important if you choose
to have the groups go to another level—that of describing
themselves in non-human terms, as:

good eraser	good advertisement
good motorcycle	good snowstorm
good chalkboard	good cat

here again, have groups make up their own "good ————"
choices and operate without your direction for a while. talk
afterwards about what it was like to do this, by writing the
following on the board and giving kids a chance to respond out
loud to any one of the choices:

i liked ————	i hope that ————
i didn't like ————	i wonder ————
i learned that i ————	i was uncomfortable ————
i'm surprised that ————	

share the books *t.a. for kids* or *t.a. for tots* with your
students. for high-school and above, distribute the workbook
entitled *winning with people.*

risk-taking

purposes

- to become aware of one's behavior in terms of risk-take and security-seeking

- to test the limits of one's individual risking boundaries

- to set up an environment where contrived risk-taking can be practiced

- to learn to be sensitive to the different degrees of risk-taking behavior present in any group *risk-taking*

definition

brainstorm behavior definition of risk-taking and its polarity,
security-seeking. give examples of risk-taking and security-
seeking

discussion starters

- how do you feel when you are risking something?

- where do you risk most often?

- "if you never risk, you can't get very hurt, but then about all
  you can say about your life at the end is: it was safe." what is
  being said or suggested here? do you agree? what are some
  other ways to say it?

- what part do 'stakes' have in each risky situation?

- what part does trust play in risk-taking?

risk-taking

circletime topics

- something that feels risky when i do it

- security is — — — —

- a big risk i took

- what i feel when i see others risking

- a risk that seems too big for me

- a risk i took and was glad

- a risk i took and was sorry

- i was afraid

- what i tell myself when i take a chance

journal entries

- a fear i've never told anyone about

- people who make me feel secure

- i hope when i take a risk i'll — — — —

- the greatest risk i could take would be — — — —

- to feel secure i would need — — — —

activities

☆

ring toss game this is an enjoyable and informative activity designed to examine risk-taking behavior.

materials needed: at least two games of indoor ring-toss (stakes can be home-made from doweling and plywood; the rings from rope and masking tape). also needed: flipchart or chalkboard. set up game areas with masking-tape markers on floor every two feet away from the stake, up to 30 feet.

there are three tasks—warmup, round 1, round 2. be sure to introduce only one task at a time without telling about future ones. each task should take about 10 minutes. introduce tasks this way:

warmup:

  in this ring toss game, you can score two points for each tape marker (2 ft.) you stand away from the stake. note that the farther away in feet you stand from the post, the harder it is, but the more points you get. for the next ten minutes, each of you take some time to practice throwing the rings.

round one:

  now, the task is to accumulate as many points as you can. each person will enter his or her name on the chart, and the distance chosen to stand from the post. each will get only five tosses. when the names and distance are set, we'll begin the round. (once recorded, distances are fixed)

round two:

  now, round two is the last and most important task. you each must better your round-one total by ten per cent. for instance,

risk-taking

if your score for round-one was 20, you now must get 22. the rules are the same, except that any person may now change the distance he wishes to stand on this round. (once begun, distances are again fixed.)

process: (in small groups, partnerships or journals)

what does the way you played the game tell you about your style of risk-taking? what were some of the feelings you experienced during this session? can you connect each feeling with an event? how did you perceive each of the other players during the game?

personal risk inventory: with the risk being 10 and security being 0, rate the following behaviors 0-10.

driving a car

flying in a plane

asking for a date

accepting a date

telling people how you feel

arguing with parents

telling your teacher you think you were treated unfairly

writing a poem and having someone read it

having your poem read aloud to the class

keeping a secret

making a promise

(how many more can you think of to add to this list)

risk-taking

☆

smile at or talk to someone you don't usually smile at or talk to.

☆

tell something you've never told

☆

make lists—

    i dare to ————

    i don't dare to ————

☆

chasm jump: place masking tape strips two feet apart on the floor. place imaginary money on one side and have kids jump over the "chasm" which they are to imagine is two feet wide and 100 feet deep—a miss means "certain death".

☆

i-dare-you game: put "i dare you" statements in a hat. pick one—do it or pass. process by dealing with feelings.

☆

6 pt. continuum: "foolish freida and fearful freddy". the extremes are the person who always risks foolishly, and the person who never takes risks.

change

purposes

- to legitimize change as a constant in our lives

- to widen students' options for behaviors as responses to change

- to increase awareness of the world as a changing place

change

definition:

write the words "change is . . ." on the board. invite students to brainstorm (a) definitions; and (b) examples. after obtaining a partial list of (b) from the class, invite students to write their own. make up a bulletin board, classbook, handout or collage out of the offerings.

discussion starters:

• how is the world different from what it was yesterday?

• how are you and i different from yesterday? from one hour ago?

• what would you do if, when you went home from school today, your house, and all the houses around it, were gone— disappeared!

• pretend that tomorrow there will be ten new students added to our class. what will this mean to you?

• evaluate this situation: someone offers you a free saint bernard puppy and you want it very much. what objections would your parents have? what would you say to change your parents' mind?

circletime topics:

- a big change for me
- something that's changing (changed) and i wanted it to stay the same
- something i'm glad is changing (changed)
- how i've changed in the last year
- how someone close to me has changed
- moving, and being in a new situation
- something that got added, that changed my life (me)
- something that got taken away, that changed my life (me)
- a change i wish would come
- a change i expect in the future
- how the world will be changed by the time i'm grown up
- a change that concerns (frightens) me
- something or someone is changing (changed), and i don't (didn't) understand it

journal entries:

- all of the above, plus these sentence stems:
- i changed my ———— and was glad (sorry)
- changing ———— seems risky to me, and here's why
- why i value change
- a change i would really hate

activities

☆

change the classroom environment: this could be done as a surprise to the class, or with their cooperation and planning (the surprise is more dynamic, and can be followed up with a planned change). some possibilities: remove all furniture for a day; readjust the temperature drastically; teacher wears a funny hat; everyone remove shoes; clock disconnected; addition of a large, bulky object such as a shrub, refrigerator carton, etc.

☆

oddly changed behavior: a day before, assign a child to act radically differently for the first hour of the next day, and to tell no one why. tell two other students about the assignment, and have them observe and take notes on interactions of other students with the roleplaying child. have them note verbal and non-verbal expressions of other kids as reactions to the change in their friend. at the end of an hour, let the class in on the secret. brainstorm feelings of all that were going on. feed back ("so you ———— when ————").

☆

change your behavior: assign kids to work in twos or threes to talk about and action-plan a small change in behavior for each. give these guidelines beforehand; discuss and answer concerns:

1. think of a situation where you always or almost always act (respond) the same way.

change

2. think *why* you act that way. list things it gets you,
   protects you from, etc.

3. think what it keeps you from, costs you, what you have
   to give up or can't enjoy because of the behavior.

4. decide on a change that would (a) get you more, or (be)
   cost you less.

5. decide on one or two small experiments (i.e. situations
   in which to try on the new way of acting), and discuss
   with your partner.

6. write a contract with your partner, naming what you will
   do, and when, to change. have your partner "notarize"
   your contract. decide on a way of rewarding yourself if
   you change successfully (preferably, a reward you can
   share with your partner). agree on a reporting date and
   system.

have students spend 30-45 minutes on this assignment,
working in their small groups, developing contracts,
discussing, etc. finish with a debrief of the exercise as an
entire class: how do you feel about what you ac-
complished? what things were going on as you were doing
this (thoughts, feelings, behaviors)? list responses on
board.

patriotism

purposes

- to understand the behavior connected with the concept of patriotism

- to accept the diversity of nationalistic views

- to be aware of the effect others make on one's allegiance to one's country

- to have more information about patriotism / revolution to make clearer decisions

patriotism

definition

- "patriotism is . . ." (synonyms)

- "patriotism is . . ." (examples)

- brainstorm a definition of patriotism which is functional for all members of your class. print it on newsprint

discussion starters

- respond: "my country right or wrong"

- how do people express their patriotism?

- when can patriotism take the form of support of government? non-support?

circletime topics

- my feelings about being american

- three things i like about my country

- three things i don't like about my country

- a choice to live in another country

- i would join a revolution against my country if _ _ _ _

- my idea of a real patriot

patriotism

journal entries

- i'm patriotic when i ————

- if i were president i would ————

- a public office i would want to have

- what i don't understand about government

- how i plan to find out about what i don't understand about government

- some revolutionary ideas that i admire

- civil rights and patriotism—what do they have in common?

- our country is hopelessly ————

- our country is rightfully ————

- america is ————

activities

☆
rank order the following:

—fame
—riches
—patriotism

—slavery
—revolution
—debt

☆

—friends
—money
—country

☆

—president
—judge
—minister

patriotism

☆ ☆

—flag
—new clothes
—savings account

—religion
—patriotism
—individual rights

☆ ☆

—bible
—constitution
—works of shakespeare

—soldier in army
—p.o.w.
—conscientious objector

process each of the rank orders or forced choice by doing:

i learned ————

i wish ————

i wonder ————

I want ————

☆

which is worst? next worst?

—fight in a war where we're supporting another country
—fight in a war against someone attacking us
—fight in a war where we are attacking

—flag being burned
—building being looted
—little kid being beaten up

patriotism

positions you would rather occupy

   —soldier
   —statesman / woman
   —policeman / woman

☆

choose best

   —march in a demonstration for civil rights
   —help with campaign for electing president
   —send $100 to CARE
   —give blood

☆

do a 6-pt. continuum on:

   amnesty

   government-controlled utilities

   federally funded education

after filling in continuums or taking stands on patriotism
issues, follow with an interview whereby you break the class into
pairs, people who are generally at extremes on the issues to gain
more understanding of each others' point of view. this is a place
where *listening skills* are crucial. in order to hear and understand
each other have them practice some paraphrasing and reflecting
of feelings.

a place where *listening skills* are crucial. in order to hear and
understand each other have them practice some paraphrasing
and reflecting of feelings.

patriotism

i'm glad i — — — —

i wonder if i — — — —

☆

do a six point continuum on:

support of government — — — — — — revolutionary

process as above.

☆

write, share or do pass-around circles on:

"america is — — — — — —"

☆

interview, on the topic "what america needs today and how we can get it":

housewife

professional woman

laborer

child

person in community government

random "person on the street"

debate the issue according to the information you collected in the interviews.

patriotism

☆

scavenger hunt: list things found in your school that show patriotic or revolutionary spirit. suggest things that should be added. decide how they will be added.

☆

collect mottos from license plates of the 50 states. try to name those which seem patriotic or revolutionary. make posters to portray the sayings you found. send copies of the posters to the state capital from which it came.

☆

how has patriotism changed? make a graph showing patriotism in the past 50 years. read about it in the time of the civil war

world war i   vietnam war

world war ii   today

korean war

☆

try to get a statement from the major politicial parties on their stands on patriotism and revolutionary spirit.

☆

plan a patriotic night with your pto, pta.

patriotism

☆

roleplay: spend a week establishing a "nation" in the classroom. try a different form of "government" each day: elected officials, inherited monarchy, revolutionary takeover, dictatorship, police state, etc. in each case, try to define "patriotic" or "unpatriotic" behavior in the governed. finally, lead the class in defining the *conditions which appear to define patriotic behavior.* under each form of government, are there any *constants?*

☆

ask the class what constitutes 'patriotism' in your classroom or the school.

joy

purposes

- to broaden students' definition of joy to include identifiable everyday experiences

- to help students to begin to see joyful experiences as ways to release human potential

- to facilitate understanding of the effect joy / sadness has on others and vice versa

- to help students practice being joyful, and to build their awareness of their own capacities for experiencing joy

joy

definition

brainstorm with the class definitions of joy. (joy is . . . joy is when . . . joy is like . . .)

discussion starters

- can you plan for joy?

- what's the experience of joy physically?

- is joy self-created or other-created?

- does joy come through big things or little things? material or non-material things?

- is joy the same as happiness? as pleasure?"

circletime topics

- the most joyful or positive thing that has happened to me during the past week

- something joyful or positive i saw someone else doing this past week

- what i enjoyed most this past week

- how i can tell when a person is feeling joy

- people who give me the most joy

- how i express joy

- the last time someone shared joy with me

joy

- a way i experience joy repeatedly

- how i'd teach someone to express joy

- how i celebrate

- what i do when someone else is joyful

- what i think we ought to celebrate

journal entries

- a positive thought which keeps coming back to me

- a great taste, visual smell or tactile experience i've had

- where i feel joy most

- i experience ———— as being full of joy

- i get joy from . . . (list)

activities

☆

in the next few minutes do something that will give you a more optimistic view. discuss with the class the different things done, the comfort level in doing these things.

☆

small groups (4-6) brainstorm the creation of a *joy machine.* then share in some way such as describing, drawing, acting out, giving a sales pitch for, etc.

joy

☆

write a play that shows how people affect others' joy; and / or how a person creates his / her *own* joy.

☆

"joymobile"—drives around town, handing out joy. give ideas, write about, construct models, or actually design.

☆

"my joyful place": all contribute. derive the components descriptions have in common. plan to introduce these, or some of these, to classroom environment.

☆

ingredients list: consider what these elements have to do with joy:

    aesthetics
    people
    common tasks
    humor
    material things
    space
    time

☆

look in the mirror and make a joyful look. where can you (do you get to) make that look?

joy

☆

"secret joygiver" game (choose names from hat, plan something to give joy to your person, *without* their knowing it).

☆

joy-a-grams—ditto off a form that students can fill out and give or send to someone to make them joyful.

☆

there are many styles of experiencing joy (i.e. yelling, crying, glowing, leaping, talking excitedly). create a bulletin board collage with pictures from media sources.

☆

six-point continuum on ways of showing joy or love. small groups share their products; then each places him/herself or the continuum.

☆

find out if anyone wants to use the "wub" to change a behavior pattern so as to experience more joy.

courage

purposes

- to have students understand the concept of courage

- to have them become aware of their own individual behavior that can be seen as courageous.

- to appreciate the effect of others on individual courageous behavior.

- to enable each to accept himself as a person with both courage and fears.

courage

definition

brainstorm "courage is . . ." and "courage is when . . ." lists.

discussion starters

- does showing courage mean fearlessness?

- how are risk-taking and courage connected?

- who is your courageous hero?

- have your students discuss the models for courage they have who are "touchable" people rather than the tv stars or sports heroes.

- list the 10 characteristics of a positive personality. ask which included "courage." discuss.

circletime topics

- a time i showed courage

- an act i consider courageous

- i wish i had the courage to . . .

- i wish i had had the courage to . . .

- i felt like a coward

- when i see someone being cowardly i usually . . .

- — — — — makes me feel like acting cowardly

- i was afraid but i did it anyway

courage

journal entires

- courage is — — — —

- when i've done something courageous i feel — — — —

- i learned to be cowardly by — — — —

- on a continuum of cowardly-to-courageous i'm — — — —

- it takes courage to — — — —

- i know i'm courageous when — — — —

- in the future, i know i'll have to have courage when — — — —

activities

this exercise is an effort at helping kids to get into the skin of a person who has done something courageous. explain to them that:

they are to get into small groups, getting ready for a role play task.

give them about two minutes to think about a person they saw or read about that did something, according to definition, courageous.

using the "first person" to describe their act, have each one take turns for their description.

101

instruct those listening to tell back to the speaker what they heard the speaker say and feel about his / her act of courage.

process by collecting:

i-learned statements
here-and-now feelings
i-wonder statements

☆

list *professions which take courage* and why.

☆

have an *advice column* where kids write anonymous letters to an imaginary columnist. solicit letters concerning courage and cowardice. make sure they get answers or directions.

☆

what do courageous people do? the purpose of the activity is to collect perceptions of the commonly accepted courageous people of the world.

have a total-class or small-group listing of all the people they can think of whom they would consider to be or have been courageous in some way.

the next task is to list by each name the things these people have done to cause us to think of them as courageous.

courage
try next to categorize these acts into:

physical acts   copping out

speaking out for a principle   running away

taking a stand   lying

helping someone   ignoring a need

others   others

process: how have you changed your mind about
courage/cowardice? who are you most like according to the
above list?

do the same exercise for "cowardly people."

☆

quiet courage: often, courage is not shown aggresively, but
quietly—as when one lives with pain or a disability without
complaint; or admits to thoughts or feelings for which he
might be blamed, made-fun-of or looked-down-upon. have
students share examples of this, from their and others' lives.

☆

make a collage of current "profiles in courage" from the news
media.

courage

☆

rank order
—risk taking
—courageousness
—daring

rank order
—being ignorant of a situation where someone needs help
—ignoring a situation where someone needs help
—lying about a situation where someone needs help

process: make sure each person who has taken a stand on the above items and wishes to, is given the opportunity to speak.

i wish i — — — —

i am more — — — — than — — — —

i like (an aspect) of my courage.

☆

profiles in cowardice: have each student write, on a ditto master, a short account of what he or she consider a "profile of cowardice". these will be collected, reproduced and made into books for sharing.

☆

yay-for-me: in *wishes, lies and dreams* by kenneth koch, the author gives somé suggestions on helping students write poetry by dealing with wishes, lies and dreams. have your students write a poem which has a lie in each line about something they did that took courage.

courage

☆

boo for me: have them write another poem or story or 'tall tale' which has to do with being a coward. *process:* try to get at the feelings of your students about things they wrote that they did as courageous or cowardly people, with

i-learned statements   i-wish statements

i'm-thankful statements   i'm-going-to statements

☆

do a six-point continuum on courage/cowardice after each "takes a stand" on it, process: if i could make a change in my courage/cowardice it would be ——————————.

intimacy

purposes

- to build appreciation for the human need for intimacy

- to help each student discover his / her style of
  intimacy / isolation behavior

- to aid students in making some behavioral choices which
  reflect an understanding of intimacy / isolation

- to begin to understand that humans are ultimately alone and
  separate even while being with others

107

intimacy

definition

brainstorm with the class a definition of intimacy. try to get consensus on what it is and isn't.

in order to circumvent the notion of intimacy being purely sexual, or between best friends, help the class broaden the definition to include the open sharing of self (even one's anger or hurt) with another, in trust.

discussion starters

- what makes a friend?

- how do you help a friend?

- how do you meet intimacy needs in a crowd? where prejudice exists? where there is demand for conformity?

- envy in our classroom and its effects

- envy has a partner, jealousy. how are they different? the same?

- what does sexuality have to do with intimacy?

intimacy

circletime topics

- how i can be intimate with myself, distant from myself

- intimacy i see in others—how they express it to each other

- unselfish love—what is it? where is it? how do you know about it?

- jealousy and my family

- i am a friend when — — — —

- i want my friends to be — — — —

- i know i have a friend when — — — —

- my style of being intimate with someone

journal entries

- i'm jealous when — — — —

- something i wouldn't tell anyone

- sex is related to intimacy when — — — —

- intimacy has nothing to do with sex when — — — —

- what i want out of an intimate relationship

- those i feel most intimate with and why

intimacy

- i feel closest to:

  boys / girls

  men / women

  people older than me / people younger

  attractive people / unattractive

  serious people / humorous people

  (brainstorm other categories with class.)

activities

☆

take pieces of rope or string 24" in length. have students choose a partner they will spend the next hour (or more) with. tie them together at the wrists. help them to concentrate on the meaning of closeness, apartness, independence, and decisions that affect them and others.

☆

take your class to a place where they have to be alone. have them spend an hour (or more) absolutely alone. one way to accomplish this in your classroom is for each to bring a sheet, cover themselves and remain covered for the designated time. debrief the concepts of isolation, aloneness, independence and the feelings that go with these experiences.

☆

in the book *loneliness: the fear of love,* the author makes this kind of statement: people choose to be lonely for several reasons. if i reach out to you and you and you accept me, what kind of commitment am i obliged to? can i exist with

intimacy

someone who really accepts me totally? on the other hand, if i reject your reaching out to me i don't have to worry about being hurt. i just choose loneliness.

have your students dicuss this concept. try to diagram it visually. recall your own experiences of choosing loneliness.

☆

have your students bring in pictures for display that depict intimacy.

☆

harry stack sullivan said that next to anxiety, jealousy is the most painful emotion a human being can feel. have students respond to this.

☆

rank order which has most effect on you—

    jealousy
    envy
    anxiety

☆

bring in a bunch of cameras (polorid works best). have people take pictures of each other. interview each other, place pictures and interview data on bulletin board.

intimacy

☆

spend 5-minutes today talking to yourself about the things you like about yourself.

☆

teacher: a good book about helping kids develop a more positive self view is: *building positive self-concepts* by donald felker. in it he talks about talking to one's self positively to enhance self concept.

☆

discussion-starter, brainstorm topic, handout or journal entry: consider this list of words:

amity	cordiality
friendliness	affection
harmony	benovelence
concord	good will
peace	familiarity

how are these the same and different from intimacy?

☆

have partners give each other a shampoo. process feelings.

☆

brainstorm reasons why touching has been given a negative label

intimacy

closeness-farness: compare touching customs in different cultures. how close may someone stand to you before it feels 'too close'? since intimacy implies closeness, what part does physical distance play? have students choose partners and present 1-minute pantomimes, skits or dialogues that depict the issue of intimacy.

☆

intimacy exercises: get bernie gunther's book on massage. have student partners do head tap.

☆

touch/don't touch: touch is one of those things our society has identified as something that could be dangerous. face it head on with the class (probably small-group, short-term rap with shared results is most effective) and discover what we are doing by saying "touch" or "don't touch" each other.

☆

touch buttons: ask: if you were wearing a button on this subject, would it say "touch", "don't touch—or what? (have students design and wear their buttons.)

☆

elevator assignment: ride an elevator and watch how no one talks or touches another. (this even happens if the people got on together.) next time you ride an elevator begin a conversation with someone like this, "what's the thing you like most about riding elevators?" role play this situation in your classroom. find an elevator to try it.

intimacy

crisis intimacy: during times of crisis people pull together. if the elevator got stuck people would talk to each other. at car accidents and fires strangers talk to each other about what's happening. how come? (intimacy is being able to relate to someone else, *without* the crisis event?)

☆

sharing myself: make a collage of things you like and don't like about yourself. share it with a partner or small group.

☆

identify a sharing behavior and practice it.

☆

isolation in the arts: isolation is not only isolation from others but may also be isolation from myself. this may not be a concept familiar to your students. discuss it in terms of self-denial. describe a person who may be isolated from self.

find pictures to show that person. write a poem about the self-isolated person. have kids collect and share records in the popular idioms that deal with this frequently-encountered theme. (suggestions: the beatles' "a fool on the hill," "a day in the life.")

☆

going beyond games: one definition of intimacy is "the willingness to risk congruence (being my own feelings, attitudes and values) with others." help your students experience this by:

114

intimacy

1. asking them to make a here-and-now wheel in journals or on paper, at the beginning of a period or day.

2. letting them spend a portion of the day, or the entire period, simply interacting as they want—visiting, sharing, milling, etc. with the following guidelines:

• keep interaction going with others

• avoid meaningless rituals ("think it'll rain?")

• talk about things that interest you

• listen to others

• try not to "play games"—impressing others with jokes, lingo, putdowns, "being cool," etc.

3. process by having them do a second here-and-now wheel. share reactions in the large groups.

☆

brainstorm ways you can practice intimacy. choose one and a person to practice with. watch for outcomes of your practice in you and others.

death

purposes

- to enable students to view death as an acceptable reality, and speak of it comfortably

- to appreciate the death experience as part of a whole rather than merely an end

- to understand the physical aspects of death

- to consider and appreciate different points of view concerning death and the hereafter

death

definition

try to write a comprehensive definition of death and life by brainstorming your students ideas of each.

discussion starters

• why we think the media concentrate so much on death

• american fixation with violence and death

• how do you feel about hunting and fishing? debate topic.

• in the physical world, how does death lead to life?

• what would the world be like if there were no death?

• how do people sometimes give up on life long before they die? how can you insure that you will "live until you die" (i.e., live fully)?

• what are people really saying when they say "i wish i were dead."

circletime topics

• i saw a dead body

• an animal died and how i felt

• i became aware of death when ————

• my fears about the supernatural

death

- styles of dying

- death and violence are — — — —

- death is ugly/beautiful because — — — —

- the worst thing about death is — — — —

- the best thing about death is — — — —

- if i didn't have to die i'd — — — —

- a time i feel most alive

- a time i feel dead

journal entries

- the closest i've been to death

- death is — — — —

- when — — — — died, i — — — —

- i hope — — — — doesn't die because — — — —

- sometimes i wish — — — — were dead

activities

☆

rank order the following professions that deal with death, from most-preferred to least-preferred:

— ambulance driver
— doctor
— undertaker
— grave yard attendant

☆

rank order ways of dying:
— drowning
— murder
— old age

—————————

— disease
— car accident
— extermination

—————————

— burning
— suicide
— suffocating
— in sleep

death

☆

read:

    american way of death
        by jessica mitford

    the loved one
        by evelyn waugh

    out—out
        by robert frost

    death in the afternoon
        by earnest hemingway

    on death and dying
        by e. kubler-ross

☆

design grave stones: perhaps following a class visit to a nearby cemetary (where rubbings of stones may be done), have students design their *own.*

☆

debate: burial or cremation?

☆

brainstorm ways we express the theme of death in our language

— in sports
— on tv
— slang uses of death
— synonyms for death

—in expressions such as:
dead wrong
deadline
kill a bottle, an idea, time
a friendship 'dies'

visit a mortuary. what's the history of this service? who makes the decisions about the disposal of the dead? find out if cremated bodies have to be dressed. why?

☆

find out about the "cost of dying" items:

— car
— organist
— coffin
— notices
— clothes
— embalming

— digging grave
— concrete liner
— plot
— insurance
— chapel rental
— other

☆

inquiries:

inquire about the training to be an undertaker.

what are the local laws concerning disposal of the dead?

how do you go about donating your body or parts of your body to science?

inquire about co-operative sea burial efforts.

find out how your city decides on places to put cemetaries.

death

☆

more discussion starters:

could there ever be a "good" reason for committing suicide? what statement does a suicide make to those he leaves behind, by his act?

should there be laws against suicide?

under what circumstances, if any, would it seem right to take a life?

☆

do a *6-point continuum* on the ways to dispose of the dead. choose a way for yourself and defend it.

☆

tell three others *when and how you will die.* (the purpose of this is not to plan your death but to discuss the event.)

☆

brainstorm the causes of suicide. study the life of someone who has taken their own life to find events which may lead to suicide.

☆

design a funeral to celebrate the decease of some repugnant rule or policy that can be changed—or, perhaps, of some negative behavior that has become a norm of the class.

death

write a eulogy or obituary of self: this exercise will get the students into saying things about themselves; their accomplishments, their impact on the world, their view of self. have them do one for now and one for 60 years from now. compare them.

☆

family deaths: most people in your class have a relative that has died. invite them to discuss the event and the effect it had on them with a small group (or write an anonymous hand-in or journal entry).

☆

share how you die daily—physically, psychologically, emotionally, etc.

☆

lay it to rest: is there a grudge, jealousy, or old feud that you would like to "lay to rest"? discuss it with three friends and together design a "funeral" for it. celebrate!

celebration

purposes

- to demonstrate the need of people to experience joy

- to broaden the definition of celebration beyond the sense of holiday

- to increase children's capacity to embrace their lives and experiences more fully

- to broaden children's skills of being happy (i.e. making *choices* to be happy)

- to build awareness and acceptance of all aspects of living

- to enrich kids' concepts of themselves and their lives

- to circumvent denial of one's experiences

celebration

definition—2 brainstorms

define: "celebration is . . . (taking life in with gladness).''

give examples: "celebration is . . . (balloons popping and horns tooting)''

discussion starters:

• people everywhere celebrate certain occasions. why is this so?

• what connections can you see between a way you celebrate and

   a fast?

   a bar-mitzvah?

   a tribal rites-of.passage?

   fraternity initiations?

   other

• what examples can we find of celebrations in the areas of:

   national history?

   birth?

   marriage?

   graduation?

   religious holidays?

   family days?

   other?

celebration

- what part does *ritual* play in celebrating?

- some people seem to have a great capacity for celebrating life. what traits are found in these people?

circletime topics:

- my favorite celebration

- how my family celebrates

- a religious celebration (what it feels like for me)

- a national celebration

- a private celebration of mine

- my style of feeling good

- three things i really appreciate

- a time i was able to turn sadness into joy

journal entries:

- my list of "i-appreciates"

- i celebrate my (something i did)

- i celebrate my (something about me)

- something i think people should celebrate

activities

☆

brainstorm: all the celebrations the class can think of

☆

plan a celebration: class (or small groups) chooses an event—
something to celebrate that is genuinely appreciated and that
would not normally be celebrated (some aspect of growth or
development, an "un-birthday," or a 'misplaced' holiday such
as "christmas in july"). plan all elements (rituals, costumes,
refreshments, decorations, etc.) and hold it.

☆

"i celebrate" session: a brainstorm in which appreciative remarks are given as public statements.

☆

"celebrity-of-the-day" (or week). plan a 3-minute
ceremony to end each class period, during which something
unique about one person in the class is celebrated. do this
until you have worked through the entire class. (ditto'd
"certificates" might be bestowed, etc.)

☆

original schoolwide celebration: have the class generate ideas
for sponsoring a celebration—perhaps of a may-day type, on
any given date—that involves the entire school in a series of
enjoyable events: the celebration should be around a theme.
(whatever it is would be up to the class, but it would preferably
have meaning for all.) the theme might deal with:

some aspect of the school's history

celebration

ecology

youth

the coming or passing of a season

a special person, family, heritage

success

music, dancing, decorations, refreshments and special events might be included. the celebration may be processed by many of the processing methods outlined in the how-to section. be sure to have children tie the elements to common celebrations they know about, pointing up similarities and differences.

☆

celebrating behaviors: be ready, with the class, to point out "celebrating behaviors" as they occur from day to day, to show that we all enjoy celebrating and do it in many informal ways (i.e. athletes slapping palms, toasts, cheering, complimenting, even smiling or winking at the right time). keep a list of these so that class can see that celebrations—formal and informal—seem to be a natural reaction to joy.

☆

teacher: an important learning for youngsters—and adults—is that normally disappointing or depressing events can *also* be celebrated. celebrating is a perfectly healthy and valid means of handling disappointments. in our society, celebration is usually tied to winning, to success. how about planning a celebration when the class *loses* a game, *can't* go on a field trip because of rain, etc. this is not cynicism, but an opportunity to *choose to be joyful.*

129

celebration

6-point continuum on "styles of personal celebration."

✩

celebrations fantasy: "close your eyes, and concentrate on your breathing for 10 full, natural breaths . . . now, tell yourself there is something in your life you are about to celebrate . . . decide what other people you want to be there . . . pick a place for the celebration that is enjoyable for you . . . what decorations, if any? costumes? food? rituals and events? concentrate on this happening—a celebration just for you—for the next 3 minutes in silence . . ." (process the fantasy by having kids share "i learned that i . . ." statements in 3s for 5 minutes.)

✩

4-person committees design and display posters celebrating

"————— day"
"up with —————"

anger

purposes:

- to demonstrate that all people experience anger

- to help kids view anger as an "okay" emotion

- to increase discrimination in kids' thinking between anger
  (an emotion, and therefore without rightness or wrongness)
  and *behavioral results* of anger (which may or may not be
  harmful, destructive and therefore wrong)

131

anger

definition

brainstrom (a) definition; and (b) examples. "anger is . . ."

discussion starters:

• what do people sometimes do when they're angry?

• brainstorm a "list of things we do with our anger"

• what things cause anger?

• what do you think people *want* when they get angry?

• how can you tell when someone is angry?

• how can you show someone else you are angry?

• how are anger and fear related, if at all? anger and hurt? anger and frustration? anger and power? anger and need?

(note to teacher: in each of the discussions, include occasional invitations like "when did *you* feel this way? what did *you* do?")

anger

circletime topics:

• a time i got very angry

• a time someone got very angry with me

• how i show my anger

• where i feel my anger

• i can name a style of anger

• what bugs me

• how the thing i did with my anger hurt someone

teacher: anger is called a 'secondary emotion'. it is a cover, and underneath the cover, is always an emotion that is tied to a more-deeply-felt need—often fear ("i'm angry because i'm afraid that . . .") if students can derive even a glimmer on this central principle about anger, they are ahead in knowing themselves.

journal entries

- my anger gets me — — — —

- my style of anger

- style of anger in my very-important-person

- list of ways my anger feels to me

- list of things i do with my anger

- underneath my anger there's — — — —

activities
☆

anger in art: each person makes a picture of his anger in varied ways and media:

collage of "things that bug me"

finger painting or paint-spraying on a surrealist mural: "anger feels . . ."

design, and wear when appropriate, buttons that portray anger feelings.

present the idea that colors on a spectrum can be "warm" or "cold", and thus matched to feelings on an anger-serenity spectrum. do something to illustrate feelings in color.

coloring black-and-white cartoon series (actual or ditto), so that the colors of characters show what they are feeling.

illustrate each of the items on the "anger is . . ." brainstorm; bind into an "angrybook."

anger

☆

pantomime guessing game: play the game using the "anger is . . ." list. a student picks one of the items and acts it out; audience guesses which item it is.

☆

feeling card game: make up a set of "playing cards" out of tagboard—enough for each player in a group of eight to have six cards (game can be played by 3 or more). write the name of a feeling from the list given below, on each of two cards. in addition, mark one-third of the pairs of cards with a symbol to designate "face"; one-third to designate "body"; and the remaining third to show "interaction." these symbols are *assignments to act out the feelings* either using facial expression, body language, or interaction using another player.

through having hands dealt, or drawing from each other (as in old maid), player in turn must briefly *pose* or *pantomime* the assignment on the card. he or she then selects another player to guess what was portrayed. if the guess is correct, each of the 2 players involved receives the card or its match from the hands of others and lays them down. if the guess is incorrect, game proceeds. winner is the person with the most cards face down, after all cards are acted and guessed. here is the list of feeling words:

anger	remorse	envy
boredom	confusion	depression
frustration	sadness	relaxation
joy	stubbornness	suspicion
disappointment	unbelieving	fatigue
pride	seductiveness	apology
anxiety	self-righteousness	loneliness
hatred	playfulness	friendliness

anger

☆

bulletin board of "anger in the news" with pictures and/or articles clipped from news media.

☆

anger flag: provide a place where a small red flag may be hoisted easily, by your or any of the students. explain that anyone is free to "raise the flag" when they want to show they are made at someone or about something.

☆

note to teacher: when anger erupts in the classroom, you can facilitate effective confrontation and winding-down through behavior that expresses these attitudes:

> it is all right to be angry—here, now. it is all right for me and it is all right for each of you. it is *not* all right to be destructive or abusive, to others or yourselves, in the anger. when one of us is angry, she or he *owns* the anger; no one else owns the anger except the person who is angry. thus, when you or i are angry, it is all right to *own* the anger, publicly—and perhaps loudly and forcefully—to the other person (anger-ee). the words to use are: "i am angry!" (or some such form of "i"-plus-feelings). this is to be done *without touching or harming the other person in any way.* as for the rest, let's be as angry as we are! and when someone *else* is angry—*listen!*

☆

i-message practice: a ditto'd worksheet on which kids are to change "you-messages" into "i-messages". example: "you bug me" = "i don't like what you're doing"; or "cut it out" = "i want you to stop that". some starter you-messages:

136

anger

you dirty coward! (change to: i think you're afraid!)

you better stop it! (change to: i want you to stop it!)

you're dumb!

if you don't get over here fast, you'll be sorry.

stupid nut to trip me like that!

you shouldn't be late.

don't ask me!

get out of here!

why did you do that?

you must be crazy to say a thing like that.

☆

note to teacher: the blaming you-message is often the prelude to violence. be on the lookout for ways to get children to own their anger to one another or to you in confrontation. say, "how can you change your message so that it tells *how you feel* right now and so that it tells *what you want* from the other person?"

☆

create a "search for the *you* in the anger-message". each morning for a few minutes, have students share items (clippings, anecdotes, jokes) in which the angry person is sending a "you-message" (blaming message—as against an "i-message" which shares angry feelings and states needs without dumping on the other person).

☆

i-want session: group students in fours or sixes, with pencils and pads. they are to take 15 minutes to call out "i wants" and

write them down individually. the advantage of the groups and
out-loud responses is the possibility of piggybacking (i.e.
being reminded by each other of variations, building on one-
another's ideas). encourage them to make as long lists as
they can in the time allotted.

next, help them code or group their i-want items into *need
categories* called: love and friendship, achievement and
recognition, leisure time, work and career, travel, education,
life and death, etc.

the following day, break groups into partnership dyads and
have them share the ways they typically react when the various
"i-wants" are not met, or are frustrated. partners brainstorm
alternatives to angry or ineffective behaviors. follow up with
"wub" worksheets.

☆

immediately after the above activity, or some other time,
initiate a discussion on the subject: *anger is tied to unmet
needs.* say: imagine a situation wherein you're not getting
what you want or need. what do you do? what do you say?
how do you look? what word or words would another person
seeing or hearing you use to describe what you are feeling?"

another level of the above discussion—and the obvious
learning objective—is to get kids to focus on alternatives to the
usual anger messages: "how could you let that other person
know what you want or need, that you're not getting?"

original pantomimes, skits, written scripts or comic-strip
activities could follow.

☆

"cold ouchies mailbox": design a box in which can be mailed bad

anger

feelings any person wants to express. periodically these are shared, collected, used as advice-columnist brainstorming, or otherwise facilitated by you. *important:* children need to understand that if they are confronting someone through the mail this way, they are to use "i" or "i feel" as alternatives to "you" or "you are" (or you-never or you-always or you-better or you-shouldn't). a sign above the mail slot could read "did you remember to change *yooz* to *eyes???*" (find another place for a "warm snugglies mailbox", for balance; in it are mailed all the positive-feeling messages: i'm glads, i-likes, i-appreciates, etc.)

☆

teacher: read *anger in the rocking chair* (lederman, j.; esalen press) and *the geranium on the window sill just died, but teacher, you went right on* (harlan quist, inc.).

☆

assertiveness training: have students sit in pairs, back to back. directions: "one of you is to say 'yes'—as if you are trying to get your partner to do something. the other is to answer 'no', as if this is something you don't want to do. do this many times, back and forth, just to see how it feels." (variations: switch tasks. switch partners. suggest kids use various tones of voice: insistent, coaxing, angry, questioning, etc.) *process* with "i learned that i . . ." statements between partners, in total group, or in journals.

☆

slap game: to get students in touch with their styles in confrontation. students are to stand in facing pairs, arms-length-apart, and raise hands. they then try to force each other off balance by slapping or pushing palms (or feinting,

making the opponent fall forward). loser is the one who
moves one or both feet (raising up on toes or heels in rocking
is not considered a loss).

have them play several rounds, then talk with partners about
"what i did or didn't do that resulted in my losing a point".
after identifying 'losing behaviors' (examples: not being
flexible enough; not watching opponent's face or eyes;
anticipating collision and falling forward; not being centered,
etc.), have them choose different partners. after similar
processing, get them to state (through sharing with partners or
in groups or in journals) *how what i did in the game is like what
i usually do when i'm in conflict with someone.* (*wub* sheets
are timely here.)

bibliography of humanistic-education cookbooks

each item on the following suggested reading list has been selected because of its eminent **usability** by classroom teachers. we call this a list of "cookbooks" because, unlike theoretical treatises on why humanistic education is a good thing, books by visionaries about why schools have to change, etc., these are books of strategies, actual recipies for making changes in your classroom day to provide for affective development. by its appearance on this list, a book qualifies as a "cookbook" in that its material can be easily:

1. adapted into a philosophical education structure we call "humanistic education" (i.e. is consistent with the assumptions listed at the beginning of this book)
2. replicated in the classroom
3. adapted to age or grade level, or to particular group needs.

141

ballard, jim. **circlebook,** mandala, 1975, amherst, mass.

berger, terry. **i have feelings,** new york: behavioral publications. 1974.

bessell, harold and palomares, uvaldo. **methods in human development-theory manual,** san diego, california; human development training institute, 1973.

borton, terry. **reach, touch and teach,** new york: mcgraw-hill book company, 1970

brayer, herbert o. and cleary, zella w. **valuing in the family: a workshop guide for parents,** san diego, california: pennant press, 1972.

brown, george isaac. **human teaching for human learning—an introduction to confluent education,** new york: the viking press, 1971.

brown, george isaac. **the live classroom,** n.y.: the viking press, 1975.

canfield, john and wells, harold. **100 ways to enhance self-concept in the classroom,** englewood cliffs, n.j.: prentice-hall, inc. 1975.

charles, cheryl i. & stadsklev, ronald. **learning with games,** an analysis of social studies educational games and simulations, boulder, colorado: the social science education consortium, inc., 1973.

chase, larry, **the other side of the report card,** goodyear pub.,pacific palisades, calif. 1975

cullum, albert. **push back the desks,** british commonwealth: harlin quist, inc. 1967

de mille, richard. **put your mother on the ceiling,** walker & co. n.y. 1967 ernst, ken. **games students play** (and what to do about them), millbrae, california: celestial arts publishing, 1972.

ginott, haim. **teacher and child,** new york: the macmillan company, 1972.

gordon, thomas. **parent effectiveness training,** new york: peter h. wyden, 1970.

——————**teacher effectiveness training,** new york: peter h. wyden, 1974.

gorman, alfred h. **teacher and learners—the interactive process of education,** boston, mass.: allyn and bacon, inc., 1969.

greer, mary & rubinstein, bonnie. **will the real teacher please stand up?,** pacific palisades, california: goodyear publishing company, 1972.

gross, beatrice and ronald, ed., **will it grow in a classroom?** delta pub., n.y. 1974

hawley, robert and hawley, isabel. **developing human potential,** amherst, ma.: education research associates. 1975

hawley, robert c. **human values in the classroom,** amherst, massachusetts: education research associates, 1973.

——————**value exploration,** amherst, mass.: education research associates, 1974.

hawley, robert c. and isabel i. **a handbook of personal growth activities for classroom use,** amherst, massachusetts: education research associates, 1972.

james, muriel and jongeward, dorothy. **born to win,** reading, mass.: addison-wesley publishing company, 1971.

johnson, david. **reaching out,** englewood cliffs, n.j.: prentice-hall, inc., 1972.

lewis, howard and streitfeld, harold. **growth games,** n.y. harcourt brace jovanovich, inc., 1970.

morrison, eleanor and mila underhill price. **values in sexuality,** n.y.: hart publishing co. inc., 1974.

osborn, alex f. **applied imagination,** chas. scribners' sons, n.y. 1963

reichert, richard. **self-awareness through group dynamics,** dayton, ohio: pflaum/standard, 1970.

sax, saville and hollander, sandra. **reality games,** new york: popular library, 1972.

schrank, jeffrey **teaching human beings, 101 subversive activities for the classroom** beacon press, boston 1972.

simon, sidney, et al,. **values clarification,** n.y.: hart publishing co. inc., 1972.

stevens, john. **awareness,** moab, utah: real people press, 1971.

thomas, marlo. **free to be . . . you and me,** new york: webster division, mc-graw-hill book company, 1974.

timmermann, tim. **growing up alive,** mandala, amherst, mass. 1975.

weinstein, gerald and fantini, mario d. **toward humanistic education—a curriculum of affect,** new york: praeger publishers, 1972.

wells, harold c., **about me,** rosemont, illinois: combined motivation education systems, inc., 1970.

other **mandala** books:

circlebook—a leader handbook for conducting circletime, a curriculum of affect

growing up alive—humanistic education for the pre-teen

parables for children over and under 21

stories with holes—inquiry training for the classroom

yearbook in humanistic education—1975

how to get to do what you've always wanted to do . . . and get paid for doing it!

also available from **mandala:**

developing human potential: a handbook of activities for personal and social growth

writing for the fun of it—experience-based approach to composition

common sense composition—helping students improve all aspect of writing

evaluating teaching: a handbook of positive approaches